Presented to:

_____

From:

_____

Date:

_____

Discovering
the
Hidden Essence
of
BEAUTIFUL LIVING

BY

J. R. MILLER

HONOR BOOKS
TULSA, OKLAHOMA

All Scripture quotations are taken from the *King James Version* of the Bible.

Beautiful Living
ISBN 1-56292-543-1
Copyright © 1999 by Honor Books
P.O. Box 55388
Tulsa, Oklahoma 74155

Edited by James S. Bell Jr.

Introduction
The Essence of a Beautiful Life

Beautiful living radiates light, warmth, happiness, and joy to all who encounter it. And the reason is both simple and profound: those who live beautiful lives have discovered the power of kindness, humility, generosity, faithfulness, compassion, and a host of other virtues that season the world around them.

Experience the fulfillment that can be yours as you, too, discover the perfect balance between a life devoted to loving God and serving others.

James Bell has gathered selections from the writings of J. R. Miller, one of the most revered authors in both America and England at the beginning of the 20th Century, into a heart-stirring collection of daily devotional readings.

Discover the essence of beautiful living in your own life.

A life does not need to be great to be beautiful. There may be as much beauty in a tiny flower as in a majestic tree, in a little gem as in a great mountain, in the smallest creature as in a massive one. —J.R. Miller

Editor's Note

When we describe something or someone today as "beautiful" we usually mean physical attractiveness. We make up our faces, clothes, and homes to be pleasing to the senses. Yet truly, outer beauty is only skin deep and of little lasting value.

In the early part of the 20th Century, J. R. Miller wrote about a beauty of an entirely different order. Inner beauty, or "beautiful living" as he describes it, goes beyond simply leading a moral or good life.

Beautiful living supersedes just being good. It is an outer-directed life with a heavenly aroma attached to it. It sheds light, warmth, happiness, and even joy to those who come in contact with it. To live beautifully means to go beyond being good and to add kindness, self-sacrifice,humility, generosity, faithfulness, compassion, and a host of other virtues that others may sweetly savor.

This beauty is grounded in a devotion to a higher ideal—a "vision of the divine" as the author calls it. As one serves God by serving others, the light of the beauty of

God's holiness shines through.

Though J. R. Miller may not be recognized today, his works published between 1880 and 1913 sold more than a million copies in Britain alone. Even then Prime Minister of England, William Gladstone, thanked Miller for his book, *The Building of Character*.

And although nothing can replace character, it can remain hidden if not directed to the benefit of others. Using our gifts with a pleasant attitude to our fullest extent in the service of others, based upon integrity, is the essence of the beautiful life. Though beauty may be in the eye of the beholder, this quality of life speaks a universal language.

If you are seeking true peace and fulfillment in daily living, the principles contained herein will not only enhance your inner beauty but help you see it clearly in those around you. This depth of living does not necessarily imply fame or greatness, at least not in this worldly sense. As the author puts it:

A life does not need to be great to be beautiful. There may be as much beauty in a tiny flower as in a majestic tree, in a little gem as in a great mountain, in the smallest creature as in a massive one. A life may be very lovely and yet be insignificant in the world's eyes.

A beautiful life fills its mission in this world and is what God made it to be, doing what God created it to do. The beauty of radiant sunsets, opulent homes, or stunning film stars may attract us, but the beauty of a life excellently lived will transform. Explore these pages and discover what it means to be a truly beautiful person.

James S. Bell Jr.

The Lord Will Provide

As you begin meditating on these devotionals, write deep in your heart this word with the strongest confidence: *Jehovah-Jireh*. This name tells you that you can trust God always; that no promise of His ever fails; that He does all things well; that out of all seeming loss and destruction of human hopes He brings blessing. You have not passed this way before. There will be sorrows and joys, failures and successes. You cannot predict your future experiences. You cannot see the next step before your feet. Yet Jehovah-Jireh calls you to trust Him calmly. He bids you put away all anxieties and foreboding, because the Lord will provide.[1]

True Living

❧ *L*ife means far more than many of us ever dream. It is not merely passing through the world with a fair amount of comforts, with enough food when we are hungry, and enough clothes to keep us warm. Life means growing into the image of Christ Himself, into His strength, into mature character, into disciplined men and women, and into the blessed peace of God. But the peace He guides us into consists of victory over all our trials, and a quietness and confidence that no external circumstances can break.

Scripture Truth

❧ *C*haracter never can be strong, noble, and beautiful, nor can conduct be worthy of intelligent beings bearing God's image, if scriptural truth is not breathed into the very soul of our personal searching and pondering of those truths. Do not stay forever in the basics of religious knowledge, amid the easy lessons learned at your mother's knee. There are glorious things beyond these: so let us go on to learn of the greater things. The Word of Christ will get into your heart to dwell and transform you only through serious thought and consideration.

Finding Our Mission

⇒ We should never be anxious about our mission in life. Nor should we perplex ourselves in the least so we try to know what God wants us to do and what role He wants us to fill. Our whole duty is to do the work of the present hour well. There are some people who waste entire years wondering what God would have them do, expecting to have their life's work pointed out to them. But that is not the divine way. If you want to know God's plan for you, do God's will each day; that, indeed, is God's plan for you in the here and now. If He has a wider sphere, and larger responsibility for you, He will bring you to it at the right time, and then you will know what will be God's plan for you and your next mission.

Prayer in Busy Days

It is in prayer that God shows His face to His children, that they have visions of His beauty and glory, that the sweet promises of His love come down as gifts into their hearts, and that they are transformed into His likeness. If you wish to be blessed, allow many seasons of prayer into your busy, harassed, tempted, and struggling life. It is in these quiet moments that you really grow. Somewhere in every stressful, frantic day get a little "silent time" for prayer. It will bring heaven down into your heart and make you strong for His service.

Sympathy of Christ

Unless words mean nothing, unless the Scriptures cheat us with symbolic images and illustrations, Christ truly feels our every grief and every struggle and sympathizes with us in each one. Remember how His heart responded to all human need when He was on earth? Sorrow stirred His compassion. Every cry of distress went to the depths of His soul. His heart is still the same. When angels are thronging around Him, and a poor, weary sufferer in some lowly home on earth or a broken, sorrowful person crouching in the darkness somewhere reaches out a trembling fingertip of faith and touches the hem of His garment, He turns around with a loving look and asks, "Who touched Me?"[2]

The Right Answers

⇌ *T*here is tremendous power in the little monosyllable "No" when it is spoken firmly and courageously. It has often been like a giant rock by the sea as it has encountered and hurled back the mighty waves of temptation. It is majestic power to say "No" to everything that is not right. But it is just as important to learn to say "Yes." There come to us offers and possibilities we must not reject and opportunities we must not throw away. Life is not all resistance and defense. We must face with a firm, strong, uncompromising "No" whatever is wrong; but whatever is right we should welcome with a hearty, cheerful "Yes."

The Disciplines of Routine

∼ *T*here is nothing like life's
drudgery to make men and women of us.
You chafe under it. You sigh for relief to be
freed from bondage to long hours, duties,
tasks, appointments, rules, to the treadmill
that never ends. Yet this is God's school for
you. It may be a cross. Yes, but all true
blessing comes to us hidden under the
ruggedness and the heaviness of a cross.
We do not grow best in easy living. Accept
your treadmill, your plodding along, your
dull tasks, and do everything well, and you
will grow in strong and noble character.

God's Giving

~ *G*od does not dole out His gifts in little portions. He pours out blessings until there is no more room to receive. He gives until our emptiness is altogether filled. He is never finished giving when you cease receiving—He still gives far more. Nothing limits the supplies we get from God except our capacity to take from Him. He would give without limit if we had room to receive that moment. The only reason we are not supplied in this glorious way, according to God's riches, is because we will not take all that God would give. The only thing that stands in the way of our being blessed to the full is the smallness of our faith.

Our Clumsy Hands

~ *M*ost of us are awkward in performing even our most loving deeds. We must learn to be patient, then, with other people's awkwardness and clumsiness. Their hearts may be gentler than their hands. Do not misinterpret their actions, judging the wrong motive where purest love is meant, indifference where affection is the warmest, insult where honor was meant. Away with petty suspicions! Be patient even with people's true faults. Let us train ourselves to discover the best in every act of others, to believe the best always of people and their actions, and to find some beauty in everything they do.

God's Better Answer

❧ God answers our prayers many
times not by bringing His will down to our
level, but by lifting us up to Himself. We
grow strong, so we will no longer need to
cry for relief. We can bear a heavy load
without asking to have it lightened. We
can bear the sorrow now and endure it. We
can go on in quiet peace without the next
blessing we thought so necessary. We have
not been saved from entering the battle we
shrink from, but we have fought it through
and have gained the victory. Is not victory
in conflict better than being freed from the
conflict? Is not peace in the midst of the
storm and the strife better than being
lifted completely above the strife?

Touching Others

There are some good people who seem to want to be friends and to do you good, but they stay at a distance and never come near you. Then there are others who draw close to you and look into your eyes and touch you. You know the difference. The former people give you only distant help, with no giving of themselves, no tender sympathy; the latter may give you less material help, but they pour a portion of their own warm heart into your soul. Christ never withheld His touch; He always gave a part of Himself. We should give the touch of Christ to others. His love should tingle in our very fingers when they touch others.

Fidelity to Duty

Too often we want to know what the result of our duty is going to be before we are ready to accept it and do it. But that is wrong, for we have nothing whatever to do with the cost or with the outcome of duty; we have to know only that it is our duty, and then go right on and do it. The true way to live is to bring to each duty that comes our way our wisest considerations and our best skill, doing what appears to us at the time to be the right thing to do, and then leaving it, never regretting nor fretting about results. God has promised to guide us. If we are living in true relationship to Him, we may expect guidance moment by moment as we go on.

Possessing and Giving

It is not having that makes us great. You may have the largest abundance of God's gifts—of money, of mental abilities, of power, of warmheartedness and leadership qualities—yet if you only hold and hoard what you have for yourself, you are not great. We are great only in the measure we use to bless others. We are God's stewards, and the gifts that come to us are His, not ours, and are to be used for Him as He would use them. When we come to Christ's feet in consecration, we lay all we have before Him. He accepts our gifts; and then putting them back into our hands, He "gave gifts unto men" and tells us to go now and use them in His name.[3]

An Eye for Flaws

We should not use our keen-sightedness to discover our neighbor's little faults. By some strange perverseness in human nature, we have far keener eyes for flaws and blemishes in others than for the lovely things that are in them. Not many of us go around talking to everyone we meet about our neighbor's good points and praising the lovely things. Many of us, however, can speak about an indefinite number of faults in many of our neighbors. Would it not be better to change this approach and begin gossiping about the good and beautiful things in others?

Silence That Is Not Golden

Is any selfishness so mean as that which holds loving and gentle words in the heart left unspoken when the dear lives of those close beside us would benefit from our words? Use your gift of speech to give comfort, joy, cheer, and hope to all around you. Use it to encourage the weary and disheartened, to warn those who are treading in paths of danger, to inspire the lethargic and discouraged ones with high and holy motives, to kindle the fires of heavenly aspiration on the cold altars of their hearts.

Christ in Us

  We should not be satisfied with only small accomplishments. If Christ dwells in each Christian, we should all be new incarnations. Christ Himself was the incarnation of God. He said, "He that hath seen Me hath seen the Father."[4] If we are Christians, we are new incarnations of Christ. We should be able to say to others: "Look at me and see what Christ is like." The beauties of Christ should be seen in us. This will become true to the degree that Christ in us is allowed to rule us and transform our lives. It should be our aim and prayer that His divine abiding in us may not be hindered, and that no part of our life shall remain unfilled.

Practical Kindness

    *K*indness must be practical, not
merely emotional and sentimental. It will
not be satisfied merely with good wishes,
sympathetic words, or even with prayers; it
should be put into some form that will do
good. There are times when even prayer is
a mockery. At times it is our duty to
answer our own requests, to be the messengers we ask God to send to help others.
We are God's messengers when we find
ourselves in the presence of human needs
and sorrows that we can supply or
comfort. Expressions of pity or sympathy
are mockeries when we do nothing to
relieve the distress.

Being and Doing

↝ *T*here is a silent personal influence, like a shadow, that emanates from everyone, and this influence is always leaving results wherever it touches another person. You cannot live a day and not touch some other life with this influence. Wherever you go, your shadow falls on others, and they are either better or worse for your presence. Our influence depends upon what we are more than upon what we do. It is by living a beautiful life that we bless the world. I do not underestimate holy activities. Good deeds must characterize every true life. We must carry out mighty works. But if your life itself is noble, beautiful, holy, Christlike, one that is itself a blessing and an inspiration, then the worth of your influence is multiplied many times.

Preaching by Shining

There is not a Christian who cannot preach sermons every day, at home and among neighbors and friends most eloquently, by the beauty of holiness in his or her own everyday life. Wherever a true Christian goes, his life ought to be an inspiration. Our silent influence ought to touch other lives with blessing. People ought to feel stronger, happier, and more motivated after meeting us. Our very faces ought to shed light, shining like holy lamps into sad, weary hearts. Our lives ought to be blessings to repair human sorrow and need all about us.

Duty at the Right Time

There is a proper time for doing the duties that are assigned to us. If we will do them in their own time, there will be a blessing to follow. If, however, we do not perform them at the right moment, we need not bother ourselves to do them at all. The time to show interest and affection to any sufferer is while the suffering is being endured, not the next day when it is over, when the person is well again—or on the other hand, dead. There are so many of us whose best and noblest thoughts are always afterthoughts, too late to be of any use! We see when it is all over what noble things we might have done if we had only thought.

Serving in Love

Work done in Christ's vineyard, gifts to missions, charities given to the poor, money given to good causes, ministries among the sick and the needy—these things please Christ only when there is love for Him in them, when they are done truly for Him, and in His name. We need to look honestly into our hearts when we crowd our days with Christian activity, to know the true spirit that prompts it all. "Lovest thou Me?" is the Master's question as each act of service is rendered, as each job is done.[5] There is no other true motive.

The Decreasing of Self

➤ *N*o grace shines more brightly in
a Christian than humility. Wherever self
comes in, it mars the beauty of the work
we are doing. Seek to do your work
quietly. Do not try to draw attention to
yourself, to make people know that you
did this beautiful thing. Be content to pour
your rich life into other wasted, weary
lives, and see them blessed and made
more beautiful, and then withdraw and let
Christ have the honor. Work for God's
approval, and even then do not think
much about reward. Seek to be a blessing,
and never think of self-advancement. Do
not worry about credit for your work or
about monuments to yourself; be content
to do good in Christ's name.

Not As I Will

We pray earnestly, pressing our very heart into heaven, but it is for the doing of our own will that we ask, not for the doing of God's will.[6] Is there a true childlike spirit when we insist on having our way with God, pushing our will without regard to His? Are we not God's children? Should we not learn obedience and submission in all things to Him? No prayer is acceptable to God which, after all its intensity and effort, is not still left to God and given to His superior wisdom. Who but He knows what is best for us?

Spiritual Greatness

piritual greatness—sanctified character, beauty of soul, the likeness of God upon our lives and hearts—shall endure forever. God wants to train every one of us into this true spiritual greatness. Many Christians grow sadly disheartened because they seem never to become any better. Year after year, the struggle goes on with the old tempers and ugly dispositions, the old selfishness, pride, and hatefulness, and they appear never to be growing victorious. Yet Christ is a most patient teacher. He never wearies of our slowness and dullness as learners. He will teach the same lesson over and over until we have learned it. If we only persevere, He will never tire of us, and His gentleness will make us great.

Patient Love

❧ "As I have loved you" means love that is sweet, fragrant, and gentle to people who are rude and mean-spirited, selfish, and full of faults, with sharp corners and only partially sanctified lives.[7] If all Christian people were angelic, and you were too, it would not be hard to love everyone; but as many other people are not yet angelic, you will still have need of patience, even if you are angelic yourself, which is doubtful.

Control of Temper

➣ *The* he worst-tempered people may
be made gentle and loving in all their
words, acts, and disposition by the renew-
ing and transforming power of divine
grace. God can take the jangled keys and
put them in tune if we will only put them
into His hand. But we must strive ourselves to be sweet-tempered. We must
watch the rising anger and quickly choke it
back. We must keep down our ugly disposition. We must learn to control ourselves,
our tempers, our feelings, our passions,
and our tongues. We must seek to develop
the gentle virtues and crowd out the
thorns. This discipline is not easy, but the
lessons can be mastered.

Forgiving Others

In the model prayer Christ gave to His disciples, He linked together divine and human forgiveness. While we pray to God to forgive our countless and enormous sins, we are taught to extend to others who harm us in little ways the same forgiveness we ask for ourselves. Let us hold no bitterness in our hearts even for a moment. Let us put away all grudges and all ill feelings. Let us remember the good things others do to us and forget the evil things. Then we can pray sincerely, "Forgive us as we forgive." If we cannot do this, I do not know how we are going to pray at all for forgiveness.

The Test of Love

❧ *T*here is a great difference between love for people you never saw and never shall see and for those with whom you mingle in close relationships. There are some persons whose souls glow with compassionate affection for the Chinese, the Hindus, or the Japanese, yet who utterly fail to love their nearest neighbors, those who jostle against them every day in business, in the pew, in the church aisle, and in society. The test of Christian love is that it does not fail even when brought into closest contact, even into friction with others.

Winning Souls

We must love those we seek to save, but we must love Christ more; we must love them because we love Christ, because He loves them, because He gave Himself for them. We must strive to win souls, not for ourselves, but for Christ. It is not sufficient to get people to love us; we must get them to love our Savior, to trust in Him, and to commit their lives to Him. We must remain out of sight. Anyone who thinks of his own honor as he engages in any Christian service is not a vessel ready to be used by Christ. We need to be careful that no shadows of our pride, our ambition, or our self-seeking, fall upon our work for Christ.

Blessings of Tribulation

When you have passed through a time of suffering and have come out of it, there ought to be a new light in your eye, a new glow in your face, a new gentleness in your touch, a new sweetness in your voice, a new hope in your heart, and a new consecration in your life. You should not stay in the shadow of the sorrow, but come out of it, radiant with the light of victory and peace, into the place of service and duty. The comfort that God gives puts deep, new joy into your heart, and anoints the mourner or the sufferer with a new baptism of love and power.

Contentment, Not Satisfaction

We must distinguish between contentment and satisfaction. We are to strive to be content in every state; we are never to be satisfied in this world, whether our circumstances are prosperous or adverse. Satisfaction can come only when we awake in Christ's likeness in the next world of eternal blessedness. We are not to seek contentment by restraining or crushing the continual cravings and longings of our souls. Yet we are meant as Christians to live amid all circumstances in quiet calmness and unbroken peace, in sweet restfulness of soul, wholly independent of the strifes and storms about us, and undisturbed by them. Content in whatever state, yet never satisfied—that is the ideal life for every Christian.

Serving Christ at Home

Many people think that work for Christ must be something outside, something great or public. They imagine that to minister to Christ they must teach a Sunday School class or join a missionary society or go out to visit sick people or go into hospitals or prisons on missions of mercy. These are all beautiful and important ministries, and Christ wants some of you to do these things as well; but the very first place you are to serve Him is in your own home. Let the blessed light of your life first be shed throughout that most sacred of all spots. Brightening that little place, you will be all the more ready to be a blessing outside. Those who are the best Christians at home are also the best elsewhere.

Keeping Our Promises

⟳ Many people promise anything you ask of them, but consider it a small matter to keep their promises. They enter into commitments with you to do this or that, to meet you or call on you at a certain time or to do some favor for you, and utterly fail to fulfill their word. This is a very serious matter to be unfaithful in keeping promises and engagements. Surely we ought to keep close watch over ourselves in this regard. We ought to be faithful to the promises we make, cost what it may. It is a noble thing when we find One whose promises we are as sure of as of the rising of the sun; whose simplest word is as good as His oath; who does just what He says He will do at the moment He says He will do it. That is the kind of faithfulness God wants.

Love As Well As Service

We may carry the belief too far that all our service for Christ, our acts of love for Him, must be also in some way acts of practical benefit and help to our fellow human beings. We may not consider all deeds and gifts wasted that do not feed the hungry or clothe the naked. In secret we may pour our broken heart's love upon Christ, bathing His feet with sorrowful tears, even though we do nothing in these acts directly for any human life. In our worship we may adore Him and love Him, though we comfort no sad heart and help no one who is weary. Nothing makes Christ so honored as our love, and surely we should sometimes just love Christ, forgetting every other person in the ecstasy of our heart's adoring Him.

God's Plan for Our Lives

God does not merely make souls
and send them into this world to take on
bodies and grow up amid crowds of other
souls with bodies, to take their chances
and make what they can of their destinies.
He plans specifically for each life. He deals
with us as individuals. He knows us by
name and loves us each one with a love as
distinct and personal as if each was the
only child He had on this earth. He has a
definite plan for each life. It is always a
beautiful plan too, for He never designs
injury and ruin for a life. He never made a
human soul for the express purpose of
being lost. God's design for each life is that
it shall attain a holy character, do a good
work in the world, fill a worthy place,
however humble, and fill it well, so as to
honor God and bless the world.

The Habit of Sympathy

The gentle ministries of love that you take time to perform as you hurry from task to task in your busy days will give you the sweetest joy as you remember them in a later moment. What these ministries are to those who receive them, you never can know till your own heart is sad and lonely and one comes to you in turn with the true comfort of love. Train yourself to attain the habit of sympathy. Be ready every hour to speak a full, rich word of love to lighten the hearts that hunger for what you have to give. God has given love to you for the very purpose of blessing those whom He sends to you day by day.

Use Your One Talent

Use your one talent for God's glory, and He will give you more to use. Do the little duties faithfully, and you will grow in skill and ability and be able for greater duties. No duties are small or unimportant. There are many who grow discouraged because they are occupied all their lives with little tasks. Men praise grand and heroic deeds, and little notice is taken of the common, heroic deeds of daily duty. But someone once said—that if God sent two angels to earth, one to rule an empire and the other to clean a street, they would each regard their employment as equally distinguished. True faithfulness regards nothing as small or unimportant.

The Cost of Being Good

We can never bless the world by merely having a good time in it. We must suffer, give, and sacrifice, if we wish to do good to others. It costs you even to simply be good. Some of us know what self-repression, self-restraining, self-crucifixion, and long, severe discipline lie behind calmness, peacefulness, sweet disposition, good-temper, kindly feelings, and thoughtfulness. Most of us have lived long enough to know that these qualities do not come naturally. We have to learn to be good-tempered, thoughtful, gentle, and even to be courteous. Learning this is always hard. Indeed we attain nothing good or beautiful in our spiritual life without a cost.

As I Have Loved You

"Love one another as I have loved you."[8] How did Christ love His disciples? How did He demonstrate His love to them? Was it not, among other ways, in wonderful patience with them—with their faults, their ignorance, their unfaithfulness? Was it not in considerate kindness, in ever-watchful thoughtfulness, in compassionate gentleness? Was it not in ministering to them in every possible way? What is it, then, to love one another as He loves us? Is it not to take His example for our pattern? But how slowly we learn it! How hard it is to be gentle, patient, kind, thoughtful, even perfectly true and just, one to another! Still, the lesson stands and waits for us, and we must never falter in learning it.

Soul Hunger

⇛ *A* religion that is satisfied with
only ordinary accomplishments—indeed,
that is ever satisfied at all—is not a living
religion. The Master's blessing is upon
those who hunger and thirst after
righteousness. It is the longing soul who is
satisfied. There are better things before you
than you have yet attained. Strive to reach
them. It is not easy to rise Christward,
heavenward, to advance in the Christian
life, to grow better. It is hard, costly, and
painful. Many people are discouraged
because they do not appear to themselves
to be any better, to be any more like
Christ, today than they were yesterday. But
even true longing is growth. It consists of
the soul's reaching Godward.

God and Nature

We talk about the laws of nature, and we say they are fixed and unchanging. Yes, but God is behind the laws of nature. They are merely His ways of working in the world. They do not work and run like a great, heartless machine; there is a heart of love, a Father's heart, at the center of all this vast order we call nature. All things work together for good to everyone who loves God. If only you keep your trust fixed upon God and are obedient and submissive, even nature's tremendous energies will never harm your inner life.

The Splendor of Ordinary Service

Every common walk of life is glorious with God's presence, if we could but see the glory in it. We are always on a mission from Christ. We have sealed orders from Him every morning that are opened as the day's events arrive. Every opportunity for duty or for heroism is a divine call. Be loyal to duty, no matter where you may hear its call nor to what service it may ask of you. Duty is necessary, however humble it may be; and duty is always noble, because it is what God Himself decrees. The work the day brings our way is always His will, and the sweetest thing in all the world to a loving, loyal heart is always God's will. The service of angels in heaven's brightness is no more radiant than the faithful duty of the lowliest saint on earth.

The Losing That Is Saving

The way to make nothing of our life is to be very careful of it, to hold it back from dangerous duty, from costly service, to save it from the waste of self-denial and sacrifice. The way to make life an eternal success is to do with it what Jesus did with His—present it a living sacrifice to God, to be used wholly for Him. Some say He threw His life away, and so it certainly seemed, up to the morning of His resurrection. But no one would say that now of Christ. The throwing away of His life led to its glory. In no other way can we make anything worthy of our life. Saving is losing. It is losing life in devotion to Christ and His service that saves a life for heavenly honor and glory.

The Value of Our Reserves

⮞ *T*here is a large difference between worrying about possible future trials and being ready for them if they should come. The former we should never do; the latter we should always seek to do. If we do, we are always prepared for emergencies, for the hard knocks, the steep climbing, the sore struggle, and we get through life victoriously. In moral and spiritual things, it is the same. It is our reserve that saves us in all the final tests— the strength that lies behind what we need in ordinary encounters. Those who daily commune with God, breathing His life into their souls, become strong with that hidden strength that preserves them from falling in the day of trial. They have a "vessel" from which to refill the lamp when its little cup of oil is exhausted.

Finding Your Mission

To find your mission you have only to be faithful wherever God puts you for the present. The smaller opportunities He gives you in the earlier years are for your training, that you may be ready finally for the larger and specific service for which you were born. Do these smaller, humbler things well, and they will prove to be steps in the stairs up to the loftier height where your "mission" waits. To spurn these simpler duties and tasks and to neglect them is to miss your important mission itself in the end, for there is no way to get to it but by these ladders of commonplace things. You must build your own ladder day by day in common, faithful acts.

The Outcome of Sorrow

~ *B*eyond the river of sorrow, there is a promised land. No grief for the present seems joyous, yet afterward it leads to blessing. There are rich possibilities for good beyond every pain and trial. There are green fields beyond Jordan's sorrows. Our disappointments are God's appointments and bring rich rewards. God takes our losses and designs them into gains for us. There is nothing really evil in the experiences of a Christian, if only God is allowed to work through the situations. Our Father sends us nothing but good. Don't worry about the package. Be it dull or attractive, it enfolds a gift of love.

A Time To Be Deaf

In the case of slander, the listener is almost as bad as the speaker. The only proper response is to shut your ears the moment you begin to hear from anyone an evil report of another. The person has no right to tell it to you, and you have no right to hear it. If you refuse to listen, he will not be able to go on with his story. Ears are made to hear with, but on occasion it is better to be deaf. We all aim at courtesy, and courtesy requires that we be patient listeners, even to dull speakers; but even courtesy may not require us to listen to evil reports about a neighbor. Ears should be trained to shut instinctively when the breath of slander touches it, just as our eyes shut at the slightest approach of harm.

Personal Influence

*Every human life has an influence in this world. Our impact perpetually continues on every side. If our lives are true and good, this influence is a blessing to other lives. Let us never set in motion any influence that we would later want buried. When we think of our unconscious, perpetual, pervading, and immortal difference in the world, we can only cry out, "Who is sufficient for these things?" How can we hope that the efforts from our lives will always be blessed? Let us be faithful in all our duties, obligations, and responsibilities, in act, word, and attitude, all our days, in whatever makes an impact. In no other way can we fulfill the responsibility of living for others.

Human Redemption

~ Christ has committed to His disciples the work of seeking, winning, and gathering perishing souls. Redemption is divine, but the accomplishment of it is human. So far as we know, no lost sinner is brought to repentance and faith except through one who already believes. It is the Holy Spirit who draws souls to Christ, yet the Spirit works through believers to unbelievers. There are those who will never be saved unless we do our part to save them. Our responsibility is based on our opportunity. Christ wants daily to pour His grace through us to other lives, and we are ready for this most sacred of all ministries only when we are content to be nothing so that Christ may be all in all; vessels emptied that He may fill them; channels through which His grace may flow.

The True Ministry of Pain

There is no Christian art of enduring pain that we should seek to learn. The real problem is not just to endure the suffering that comes into our life, to bear it bravely, without wincing, to pass through it patiently, even rejoicing in it. Pain has a higher mission to us than to teach us heroism. We should endure, seeking the blessing of it: a message from God that we should not fail to hear. It lifts for us the veil hiding God's face, and we glimpse His beauty every time we are called to suffer. Pain is like a furnace fire, and we should come out of it always with the gold of our character gleaming a little more brightly. Every experience of suffering ought in some way to lift us nearer God, to make us more gentle and loving, and to leave the image of Christ shining a little clearer in our lives.

Faultfinding

It is strange how oblivious we can be of our own faults and of the blemishes in our own character, and how clearly we can see the faults and blemishes of other people. Finding so much wrong in others is not a flattering indication of what our hearts contain. We ought to be very quiet and modest in criticizing others, for in many cases we are merely telling the world what our own faults are. Before we turn our microscopes on others to search out the less than beautiful things in them, we had better look in our mirrors to see whether or not we are free ourselves from the blemishes we wish to correct in our neighbor. There is a wise portion of Scripture telling us to get clear of the beams in our own eyes, that we may see clearly to pick the specks out of the eyes of others.

Making Sweet Memories

We are all making memories today for our tomorrows. The rear log in the fireplace sings as it burns, and a poet once said the music is the birdsongs of past years. When the tree was growing in the forest the birds sang in its branches, and the music sank into the tree and was held there, until now in the winter fire it is set free. This is only a beautiful fancy, but the analogy has truth. In the days of childhood and youth, the bird-notes of gladness sing about us and sink away into the heart to hide. In busy days of toil and care, they may be lost and forgotten. Later, the fires of trial come and inflame our lives with the long-imprisoned music set free and flowing out. Old age can be brightened by memories of early years. The wise fill their hearts with pure, pleasant things in their youth and lay up blessings for old age.

In All Your Ways

Do we make much of God in
our lives? Is God really special to us in our
conscious personal experience? Do we go
on making plans and carrying them out
without once consulting Him? We talk to
Him about our souls and about our spiritual affairs; but do we speak to Him about
our daily work, our trials, our perplexities,
our weekday, work-a-day life? Do we shut
God out of part of our life? We must have
something beyond our human nature,
even at its best, if we would be ready for
all that lies before us. We must allow our
small lives to get so attached to God's big
life that we can draw from His fullness in
every time of need.

The Blessing of Temptation

We sometimes wish there were no temptation, no difficult trial in life, nothing to make it hard to be good, to be true, to be noble, to be pure. But did you ever think that these great qualities can never come easily, without struggle, without self-denial, or without toil? Every promised land in life lies beyond a deep, turbulent river, which must be crossed before entering the beautiful land. Not to be able to cross the stream means we are not able to enter the blessed country. Every temptation is a path leading to something noble and good. If we endure the temptation and are victorious, we shall find ourselves within the gates of a new paradise. "Blessed is the man that endureth temptation: for when he is tried, he shall receive the crown of life, which the Lord hath promised to them that love him."[9]

Fidelity in Trifles

There will be eternal honors for those who have filled important places of trust and responsibility in this world and have proved faithful in great things. There will be crowns of glory for the martyrs who, throughout the ages, have died rather than deny Christ. But there will be rewards just as brilliant and crowns just as splendid for those who, in lives of lowly service and self-denial and in patient endurance and humble devotion, have been faithful in the small things. God does not overlook the lowly, nor does He forget the little things. If only we are faithful in the place to which He assigns us and in the duties He gives us, we shall have our reward, whether the world praises, or whether our lives and our deeds are unknown and unpraised by others. Faithfulness wins the approval that brings glory.

Power and Responsibility

*Power leads to responsibility. You are not responsible merely for what you are trying to do, but for what God has given you power to do. Wake up those slumbering possibilities in your soul; you are responsible for all of them. Stir up the unused, inactive gifts that are in you; you are responsible for these as well. The things you can do, or can learn to do, are the things Christ is calling you to do, and the things He will require from your work when He comes again. It is time we understood life's meaning. God gives us seeds, but He will require more than seeds from our work; He will require all the harvest of beauty and blessing that the best cultivation can bring out of the seeds.

The Ministry of Sympathy

No ministry in this world is more beautiful or more helpful than that of those who have become familiar with life's paths, and have learned life's secrets in the school of experience, and then go about inspiring, strengthening, and guiding younger souls who follow them. Nothing in Christ is more precious than this knowledge of life's ways, gained by His own actual experience in walking this earth. He has not forgotten what life was like back then. He remembers how He felt when He was hungry, or weary, or in struggle with the tempter, or forsaken by His friends. And it is because He went through all these experiences that now in heaven He can be touched with the feeling of our infirmities and can give us sympathy, help, and guidance.

Growing Through Good Habits

One whose daily life is careless is always weak; but one who habitually walks in the paths of uprightness and obedience grows strong in character. Exercise and practice develop all the powers of his character. Doing good continually adds to his capacity for doing good. Victory in trial or trouble puts new strength into his heart. The habit of faith in the darkness prepares for stronger faith. Habits of obedience make one unshakable in one's loyalty to duty. We can never overestimate the importance of life's basic habits; they direct our growth in character in whatever way they point toward.

Your Will Be Done

God's will for us leads on earth to the noblest, truest, most Christlike character, and then beyond this world to glory and eternal life. For you, whatever your experiences, however hard and painful life may seem to you, God's will is the very hand of divine love to lead you on toward all that is good and beautiful and blessed. Never doubt it, even in the darkest hour, or when the pain is the greatest, or when the cross is heaviest. God's will always holds you close to God, and leads you continually toward and into God's sweetest rest. It brings peace to the heart—a peace that never can come in from our own choosing—to always be able to say, "Thy will be done." [10]

Love's Ministry

Love's quality is measured by what it will do, what it will give, and what it will suffer. God so loved the world that He gave—gave His only begotten Son, gave all—and withheld nothing. That is the measure of the divine love for us: it loves to the uttermost. If you are Christ's, every energy of your mind, every affection of your heart, every power of your soul, every fiber of your body, every element of your influence, every penny of your money, is Christ's, and all of these are to be used to bless others and to make the world better and happier. If we love, we will give, we will suffer, we will sacrifice. If we would be like God, we must live to minister to others, giving our life, without reserve, to service in Christ's name.

Before the Sun Goes Down

≈ *C*onflicts between friends should not be permitted to continue overnight. Scriptures say we should not let the sun go down on our anger. Why? Because there may not be another day to heal the wound and fix the broken relationship. "But it was not my fault," you say. Noble souls, inspired by the love of Christ, must not look for blame nor argue who should first seek restoration. If it was not your fault, you are the better person to begin the reconciliation. It is Christlike for the one who is not to blame to take the first step toward the healing of the breach. That is the way He did and always does it with us. Do not delay any longer. Is the sun close to setting? Before the evening shadows, be reconciled with your friend. Let not the stars look down on two hearts split apart by anger or misunderstanding.

Greatness in God's Sight

No one is endowed with all gifts. Everyone has his or her own particular excellence or ability. No two have precisely the same gifts, and no two are called to fill precisely the same place in life. The role of the lowliest and the humblest with the fewest gifts is just as important as the most brilliantly gifted. The great life in God's sight is not the prominent one, but the life that fills the place it was made to fill and does the work it was made to do. God does not ask great things; He asks only simple faithfulness, the quiet doing of what He commands.

Minor Lies

≈ *T*here are other forms of untruth-
fulness besides the direct lie. There are
those in our society who would not speak
an untrue word, who still twist their state-
ments so as to make them false in the
impression they leave with others; or they
would not speak a lie, but they will live
one. Their lives are full of small deceits,
concealment, pretense, insincerity, and dis-
honesty. Be true in your inmost soul—true
in every word, act, look, tone, and feeling.
Never deceive anyone. There are no white
lies in God's sight; it is a terrible fiction to
think there are.

Today, Not Tomorrow

There are duties that must be done at a particular moment or they cannot be done at all. It is today the sick neighbor needs your visit and your help; tomorrow he may be well or others will have ministered to him, or he may be dead. It is today that your friend needs your sympathy, and your comfort; it will not be of any use to her tomorrow. It is today that a tempted person needs your help in his struggle; tomorrow he may be defeated, lying in the dust of shame. It is today you must tell the story of the love of Christ, tomorrow it may be too late. Learn well the meaning of "now" in all of life. Tomorrow is a fatal word; thousands of lives and countless thousands of hopes have been wrecked by it. Today is the time of divine blessing.

Trusting for Tomorrow

Should the uncertainty of all human affairs sadden our lives? No; God does not want us to allow tomorrow's possible clouds to shadow today. He does not want us to be unhappy while the sun shines, because by and by it will be dark. He wants us to live in today and enjoy its blessings and do its work well, though tomorrow may bring calamity. How can we? Only by calm, quiet, trustful faith in God and obedience to Him at every step. Then no troubled tomorrow can ever bring us harm. Those who do God's will each day, God will hide under His wings when the storm breaks.

The Beauty Within

☞ *B*odily health is beautiful.
Mental vigor is beautiful. But heart purity
is the glory of all loveliness. The heart
enshrouds the life. The inner life fashions
the outer life. So, above all things, be pure-
hearted and let Christ more and more into
your life, that He may fill all of your soul,
and that His Spirit may permeate all of
your being. Then the beauty of the Lord
may be upon you, and the winning charm
of God's loveliness may shine in your
features, and you will have the beauty
of Christ within you. The transfiguration
must come from within. Only a holy,
beautiful heart can make a holy,
beautiful character.

Answers That Await

The day may come to us when we shall cry to the Lord, and He will not seem to hear. Whenever this experience may come, let us remember that Christ's silence is not a refusal to bless. There may be some problem in ourselves, and a work of preparation is needed in us before the blessing can come. Instead of doubting or blaming the Master, we should look within ourselves and ask what it is that keeps His answer from us. When we are low in the dust of humiliation, when our weak faith has grown stronger, when our self-will is gone, and we are ready to receive the blessing in God's way and in His time, the silence will be broken by God's most gracious answer.

Character Building

⇒ *T*he symbol of the silent temple-builders on Mount Moriah is the picture of all the worthwhile work within us. The builders are always at work on our characters, but they work quietly. The little blocks come from a thousand sources and are laid upon the walls of our hearts. The lessons we receive from others, the influences friends exert upon us, the books that feed our minds, the impressions our experiences leave upon us, the inspiration from the Holy Spirit—in all these ways the quiet work of building goes on. It never ceases, because the builders never rest. By day and by night, your character-temple is rising. Is it completely beautiful? Are the stones all clean and white? Let the builders finish their work.

Strongest with the Weakest

We are not all equally prone to temptation. There are some with a sweet temper and sweet disposition whom nothing disturbs. God seems to have sheltered them by their very nature from the power of evil. Then there are others whose natures seem to be vulnerable on all sides, exposed to many dangers. Just to survive truly brings them fierce struggles every day. These easily tempted ones receive Christ's sympathy and help in the most tender manner. He singles out each one from every walk of life that is most liable to fall, and makes special intercession to the Father for that one. Even those like John, with their gentle loveliness, need less help from the Master than do the fiery Peters.

Weakness of Little Faith

It is because of our lack of faith, or our small faith, that there are so little results from our ceaseless rounds of activity. If we had the power of Christ resting upon us as we should have, then even with only one-tenth of the activity there would be ten times the results. Think of the possibilities of our lives—the simplest, common ones, if we had all of Christ— what might be accomplished! He is ready to do greater things through us than He Himself did. We need faith to put ourselves in Christ's hand as the chisel is placed in the hand of the sculptor. Then every influence of ours will produce beauty in some life. Then all the power of Christ will work through us.[11]

The Sanctity of a Consecrated Life

The soul that has had a vision of the Christ, the person in whom Christ is already formed the "hope of glory," and who is also himself destined to wear the divine image, must never drag his reputation in the dust of sin, and must never degrade his holy life in any evil doings. Every time we are tempted to commit some sin, if we would stop and think, "I am now a child of God; shall a child of God, destined to wear Christ's image, stoop to be untrue or dishonest or impure, or to indulge in wrath or bitterness?" Should we not turn away from temptation? Could we sin against God with the awareness of our high calling in our heart?

The Law of Amusements

Amusements are proper only so far as they make us better Christians. Whenever they become hindrances to us in our Christian living or in our progress in sanctification, they are harmful, no matter how innocent they may be in themselves. How do your amusements affect your spiritual life? What is their influence on you? They may be very pleasing to you and provide great pleasure. But what is their influence on you as a Christian? In other words, are they means of grace? Or are they making you careless regarding Christ and hindering your advancement in spirituality? We ought to be honest enough with ourselves to answer these questions truthfully and then act accordingly.

The Eloquence of Living

Tongues of angels without love to inspire their silvery melody are but tinkling cymbals. Life itself is infinitely more striking than speech. Character far surpasses strong speeches as a force for change in this world. The standard of words is a false one in the estimating of the value and power of Christian workers. Do what you have gifts to do. Be sure that your heart is in it. Make your personal character a strong force in the world. Then when the sounds of silvery speech have died away, your influence will still remain a living legacy in the hearts of everyone and an unfading light in the world.

What to Do with Injuries

~ Shall we seek vengeance for the wrongs, injuries, and injuries inflicted upon us by others? How are these wrongs to be righted, these injuries to be healed? Do not fear the consequences of any wrong done to you. Simply put the matter into God's hands and leave it there, and He will make it all clear as the noonday. He will not allow us to be permanently and completely injured by any injury. Our duty, then, is to bear meekly and patiently the suffering others may cause us to endure; to bathe with love the hand that strikes us, to forgive those who injure us; and to commit all the injustices, wrongs, and inequities of life into the hand of a righteous and just God. The oyster's wounds become pearls; and God can bring pearls of spiritual beauty out of our hurts.

Learning Meekness

Religion is not sound believing only; it is receiving the good things written by good men and women of God out of the old pages of inspiration where we find them and into our own lives. Meekness as a beatitude is very beautiful. Meekness in Moses we admire greatly. But how much of it are we getting out of his life story into the experience of each common day? In our daily relationships with others, do we keep our hearts quiet and still under all harsh, rude, critical, and unjust behavior? There are countless little irritations and provocations that create friction every day. How do we endure them? Do they polish and refine our natures? These are the lessons of meekness.

Silence That Is Golden

It is easy for one to poison a person's mind concerning another's reputation. There is measureless ruin created in this world by the slanderer. Characters are blackened, friendships are destroyed, jealousies are aroused, homes are torn up, hearts are broken. Let us never take up an evil report and give it life on our own. Let us never whisper an evil word about another. We do not know where it may end, how it may grow, or what ruin it may work. Words once spoken can never be taken back again. We'd better learn to keep the door of our lips locked and speak no evil of anyone.

The Shadow of God's Wings

Is there a grief in your heart that grows into a nagging pain? Is there a hint of a coming sorrow that you see looming over you? Remember it is the shadow of God's wings, and so it is safe to receive. Crawl closer under it. Earth has nothing so gentle as true mother-love; but God's wings that fold down over you are gentler than even mother-love; and you can never get out from beneath them. They hold you close to the gentle heart of the divine Father. You need never be afraid while resting there. In all the universe, there is no harm that can come near you. From your eternal shelter, you can look out with confidence from a window of heaven on the fury of earth's storms and be at peace. The wildest of them cannot touch you in your shelter.

The Beauty of Religion

While the Christian life is firm and yielding in its integrity and uprightness, it is still beautiful in its love and gentleness. The unchangeable principles of uprightness, like mountain-crags, are covered over with tender vines and the sweet flowers of grace and charity. True religion is never meant to dry up our life and make it cold, hard, and dead. It is meant to bring out new beauty, to clothe the soul in garments of loveliness. It asks for the development of every power of body, mind, and spirit to the greatest possibility. It demands the strongest motives for goodness. It demonstrates the finest examples. Its ideal includes not only "whatsoever things are true, whatsoever things are just," but also "whatsoever things are lovely."[12]

Self-Renunciation

*T*hey are the highest quality of those who serve, who live for others, whose lives are spent in loving, unselfish ministry; and they rank highest of all who serve deeply and unselfishly. It is only in serving that we begin to be like the angels and like God Himself. It is when the worker for Christ utterly forgets herself, and sacrifices herself in the fire of her love for Christ, that her labor for souls yields the richest and best results. When we care only that Christ may be magnified, whether by honor or dishonor, whether by life or death in us, then will He honor us by using us to win souls for His kingdom.

Saying "Yes" to Christ

To believe on Christ as a disciple is to say "Yes" to Him always, with our whole heart, and with our whole being. It means giving up the sins that grieve Him. It means cutting free from whatever displeases Him. It is renouncing every other master and taking orders from Him only. It means walking with Him, following Him wherever He leads, without question, without reservation, not counting the cost. It is saying "Yes" to Christ whatever He may ask us to do or to give up or to sacrifice or to suffer. That was the way His first disciples followed Him. And that is the way His disciples must follow Him now. Absolute obedience to Him is the condition of following Him completely.

His Love Endures

⮞ The most wonderful fact in the universe is our Savior's love for His own redeemed ones. Christ bears with all our infirmities. He never tires of our inconsistency and unfaithfulness. He goes on forever forgiving and forgetting. He follows us when we go astray. He does not forget us when we forget Him. Through all our stumbling and sinning, through all our provocation and disobedience, through all our waywardness and stubbornness, through all our doubting and unfaithfulness, He still clings to us, and never lets go. Having loved His own, He loves to the end.

Divine Providence

In divine providence, nothing comes a moment too soon or too late, but everything comes in its own complete time. God's clock is never too slow. Every link of the chain of God's providence fits into its own place. We do not see His providence at the time. Not until afterward will you see that your disappointments, hardships, trials, and the wrongs inflicted on you by others, are parts of God's good providence toward you, and full of blessing. Not until afterward will you see it, but the "afterward" is secure if you firmly and faithfully follow Christ and cling to Him. The "afterward" of every disappointment or sorrow is blessing and good. We only need to learn to wait in patience for Him.

Victory by Yielding

Jacob had victory and blessing not by wrestling, but by clinging. His limb was out of joint and he could struggle no more, but he would not let go. Unable to wrestle, he wound his arms around the mysterious opponent and held on until at last he conquered. We do not get victory in prayer until we cease struggling, give up our own will, and throw our arms about our Father's neck in clinging faith. Human strength cannot take blessing from God. It is never the strength of our willfulness that prevails with God, but rather clinging faith. It is not when we press and seek our own will, but when humility and trust unite and say, "Not my will, but thine."[13] We are persuasive with God only to the degree that self is conquered and is dead. Not by wrestling, but by clinging, do we get the blessing.

The Lesson of Peace

Wherever Christ places us, we are to stay; and where He sends us, we are to go. In the heat of life's conflicts, obstructed by a host of things that tend to distract our peace, we are to maintain an unruffled calm and the tenderness and simplicity of the heart of a little child. That is the problem Christ presents to us, but He will help us if we accept Him as our teacher. As the tender grass and even the sweet flowers live and thrive all through the winter under the deep snows and emerge in the springtime in beauty, so our hearts may remain loving, tender, and joyous through life's severest winter under the snows of trial and sorrow.

Climbing Higher

Someone asked an old minister where repentance was. "The first turn to the right," was his answer. If you want to grow in Christlikeness, rising finally into radiant purity and sainthood, you must begin with the first simple duty that comes to you. Resist the first temptation. Do the first thing that occurs. Accept the first vision of divine loveliness you see. You cannot reach sainthood at a one-step, you must conquer your way up through many.

Always Our Best

All Christ asks from any of us is what we have the ability to do. He asks no impossibilities apart from His grace. He accepts our smallest, poorest gifts or services if they are indeed our best and if true love toward Him consecrates and sanctifies them. We need to care only for two things—that we always do our best, and that we do what we do through love for Christ. If we are faithful to the measure of our ability and opportunity and if love sanctifies what we do, we are guaranteed of our Lord's approval. But we should never offer less than the best that we can do; to do so is to be disloyal to our Lord and disloyal to our own soul.

Think No Evil

    Love does not suspect
unkindness in kind deeds. It does not
imagine an enemy in every friend. It does
not fear insincerity in sincere expressions
of love. It does not question one's motives
nor discount their acts. But love overlooks
mistakes and hides human faults. It
believes in the good that is in people and
tries to think of them always at their best,
not at their worst. It considers the best
possibilities in people, what they may
become through divine love and grace and
not merely what they now are. It is wonderful how seeing through love's eyes
changes the whole view of earthly life,
transforming it. If the heart is filled with
suspicion, distrust, and doubts, the world
grows very ugly. But love sees brightness,
beauty, and hope everywhere.

Darkness Reveals Love

Whatever makes us forget ourselves and think of others lifts us heavenward. This is one reason that God permits suffering. We would never know the best and richest of human love if there were no pain, no distress, no experience of grief or of need. The best and holiest mother-love would never be manifested if the child never suffered. The same is true of God's love. God would have loved His children unfallen just as much as He loves them fallen now, but the world would never have known so much of God's love had not man fallen. Our great need called forth all that was richest, holiest, and heavenly in our Father's heart. If there were no night, we would never know there are stars. Darkness reveals the hidden things.

Faithfulness

Whatever your duty is, you cannot be faithful to God unless you do your work as well as you can. To neglect it is to rob God. The universe is not quite complete without your small job well done. "Be faithful" are the words that ring from heaven in every ear, in every small assignment of work we are doing. "Faithful" as a measuring stick is not a pillow for laziness. It is not a lowering of one's obligations to make life easy. Faithfulness is a lofty standard. It means our very best always. Anything less is unfaithfulness.[14] The universe itself suffers, and the smallest duty is not done or badly done and leaves a vacuum and a blemish on the whole world's work.

Blessed to Be a Blessing

God blesses you that you may be a blessing to others. Then He blesses you also a second time in being a blessing to others. The talent that is used multiplies. Receiving, unless you give in return, makes you full and proud and selfish. Give out the best of what you have in the Master's name for the good of others. Lend a hand to everyone who needs it. Be ready to serve—at any price—those who require your service. Seek to be a blessing to everyone who comes, if only for a moment, under your influence. This is to be similar to an angel. It is to be Christlike. We are in this world to be useful. God wants to give His gifts and blessings through us to others. When we fail as His messengers, we fail in our mission.

God Himself Is
His Own Best Gift

Enlarge your desires and your prayers. Do not ask merely for mercies and favors and ordinary gifts. Do not ask God merely to give you bread and health and friends and prosperity. Do not content yourself with asking for grace to help in temptation or for strength to fill up your weakness or for wisdom to guide you in confusion or for holiness and purity and power. Ask for God Himself, and then open your heart to receive Him. If you have God, you have all other gifts and blessings in Him. God is willing to give you Himself for the asking, not merely the favors and benefits that His hand provides. Ask for great things.

A Beautiful Life

A life does not need to be great to be beautiful. There may be as much beauty in a tiny flower as in a majestic tree, in a little gem as in a great mountain, in the smallest creature as in a massive one. A life may be very lovely and yet be insignificant in the world's eyes. A beautiful life fulfills its mission in this world and is what God made it to be, doing what God created it to do. Those with only common gifts are in danger of thinking that they cannot live a beautiful life, cannot be a blessing in this world. But the most obscure life that fills its place well is far lovelier in God's sight than the grandest and most splendidly gifted life that still fails in its divine mission.

Following Our White Banners

Consecration to God is nothing less than doing the will of Christ rather than our own, doing it always, whatever the cost, the sacrifice, or the danger. There is too much mere pretense in our religion. We say we believe in Christ; but if we do, we must follow Him wherever He leads, though we don't know where. We say we love Christ, and from His lips comes the crucial test. "If ye love me, keep my commandments."[15] To be a Christian is to be devoted utterly, and irrevocably, to Christ. Joan of Arc said the secret of her victory was that she commanded her white standard to go forth boldly; then she followed it herself. Good intentions and vows and pledges of consecration are seen as white banners. But when we have sent them forward, we must be sure to follow them ourselves.

Strength in Time

There is no promise of grace before you need it. God does not say He will strengthen our arms for the battle when there is no battle. When the conflict is approaching, we are given the necessary strength. He does not open the gates for us nor roll away the stones until we come to them. He did not divide the waters of the Jordan while the people were still in their camps nor even when they began to march toward the river. The wild stream continued to flow even as the feet of the priests dipped in the water. This is the continual law of God's divine help in time of need. It is not given in advance. As we come to the need, the supply is ready but not before. Do not worry because you cannot see the way clear and the needs supplied far in advance of your steps. Let God provide and have faith in Him.

Turning Visions into Life

God gives us visions of spiritual beauty so that we may turn them into reality in everyday life. We should bring down and transform all our heavenward aspirations into acts. All our longings and desires should be made true in our experience. Every day's Bible text should be taken into the heart and should shine forth tomorrow in some new aspect of spiritual beauty. As the look of one's face is captured in a camera and held there, in the same way every time Christ looks upon our souls, even for an instant, some impression of His features remains there as part of our own spiritual beauty. We hear in all our life, the lessons we are taught, and the holy influence that touches our souls, the words of Christ, and they should enter into the soul of our being and reappear in our attitudes, character, and deeds.

Other People's Faults

❧ *I*t is easier to see other people's faults than our own. Are we troubled more about the way our neighbors live than we are with our own shortcomings? We display more responsibility for the failures of others than for our own. Yet, everyone must bear his or her own burden. We shall not be called to answer at God's judgment seat for the deeds of others. Rather, we shall give account for our every act, word, attitude, and feeling. We should train ourselves to keep a conscientious watch over every aspect of our own life. It is better to give less attention to our neighbor's foibles and failures and more to our own. If we give strict attention to our own faults, there is little time to look after other people's. Seeing and knowing our own defects makes us more charitable to those of others.

The Fatherhood of God

How it would brighten and bless our lives if we were to always keep in our hearts the concept of God as our Father! When we can look up into God's face and say out of a warm and responding heart, "Our Father," all the world and all life take on a new appearance before our eyes. Duty is no longer hard nor a drudgery, but becomes a joy. Keeping the commandments is hard if we think of God merely as a King; but if we look up to Him as our Father, everything is changed, and our life for Him and our desire to please Him make obedience a joy. We can then say, "I delight to do thy will, O my God."[16]

In the Discouraging Days

⇝ We all have our discouraging days, when things do not go well. Young people fail school lessons although they have studied hard and done their best. Homemakers and executives grow tired. Parents struggle to control their children. It may seem impossible to keep a good perspective, to maintain a loving disposition so essential to a pleasant day. Try as you will to be gentle, kind, and patient, your mind is clouded. You come to the close of a long, unhappy day disturbed, defeated, and discouraged. You have done your best, but you feel like a failure. You fall upon your knees with only tears for a prayer. Lift up your eyes and see who will help. Before His sweet smile the shadows flee away; at His Word new strength is given. Your work is easier, and life is better again.

Blessing in Mistakes

     If we repent of our mistakes and sins, they will be used by God to help in the growth and upbuilding of our character. Even when we fall, through the grace and tender love of Christ, these become new births. In the hot fires of repentance, we leave behind the dross and come out again as pure gold. But we must remember that it is only Christ who can make our sins turn into blessing. If we are Christ's true followers, even our defeats shall become blessings to us, stepping-stones on which we may climb higher. This is one of the marvels of divine grace, that it can make all things work together for good.

Speak Out the Loving Words

How much better would it be if we were more generous and lavish of our good words when our friends can be cheered and blessed by them! Sometimes we get the lesson of keeping silence over-learned, and let hearts starve for lack of kindly words that lie meanwhile on our tongues ready to be spoken. It is not the want of love for which we are to be blamed, but the stinginess that locks up the love and will not give it out in word and act to bless hungry lives. Is there any miserliness so mean? We let hearts starve close beside us when we have the bread to feed them, and then, when they lie in the dust of defeat or death, we come with our love to speak eloquent funeral eulogies. Would it not be far better to give out kind-liness when it will do good?

Christian Work

Bring every virtue and gift of your life to Christ's service. Use well the gifts you have at work now, and develop what you have into greater skill and power for service. Strive always to excel. Grow by working. Don't stand with idle hands for a moment, because you must give account for each moment. Do not allow your spiritual power to rest in dusty niches merely to look at. Take them all down and put life into them, that they may be useful. Do not play at Christian work. The King's business requires haste.

Character Alone Abides

We must strive to realize every dream of goodness and Christlikeness that our hearts seek. Remember that it is character that is the only test, and the only true fruit of living. It is not knowledge; for knowledge will fail. It is not money; for money cannot be taken away from earth. It is not fame; for fame's laurels fade at the grave's edge, and its voice cannot be heard in the valley of shadows. It is not culture or education or refinement either. It is life—not what we have or what we know, but what we are—that we can carry with us into the eternal world.

Home Friendships

≈ *F*riendships in each family require the most gentle care and cultivation. We must win one another's love within our own doors just as we win the love of those outside—by the sweet acts and virtues of affection. We must prove ourselves worthy of being loved by those who are nearest to us; they will not truly love us merely because we are of the same household unless we love them. We must show ourselves unselfish, thoughtful, gentle, and helpful. Home friendships must be formed as all friendships are formed—by the patient knitting of soul to soul and the slow growing of one life into another life. Then we retain other friends—by a thousand little winning expressions of love. We must be watchful of our acts and words.

The Heart's Daily Bread

We all need sympathy, human kindness, cheer, fellowship, and the thousand little expressions of human love, as we go along the dusty road of life. These small tokens of affection are the bright side of every life that is blessed by rich friendships. It is this unceasing blessing that your heart hungers for as its daily bread—not great gifts and large favors, but a gentle affection in your friend to bring cheer, comfort, inspiration, hope, and strength to your soul every time you look into His face.

In His Name

If we have the true spirit of service, we will look upon everyone we meet, even casually, as one to whom we owe some debt of love, one sent to us to receive some blessing, some cheerful word, some comfort, some strength, some inspiration, some touch of beauty from our hand. We may never do even one great or noticeable thing that people will talk about or that will be reported in the newspapers. Yet every word we speak, every small act, every influence we bring out, even unconsciously—all "in His name,"[17] meeting human need and pain and sorrow as we pass by—will prove to be a sweet and blessed ministry of love and will impart strength and help to others. The name of Christ consecrates every smallest deed or influence, pouring it full of love.

I Say What I Think

↬ Some people boast of their honesty and frankness because they "just say what they think," flinging out the words right and left as they come, no matter where they strike or whom they wound. Do not call it honesty, this boastful frankness; call it rather miserable rudeness, reckless cruelty. We have no right to say what we think unless we think lovingly and sweetly. We certainly have no right to unload our jealousies, envies, bad tempers, and miserable spite upon our neighbor. If we must be bad-tempered, we should at least keep the ugliness locked up in our own breast, and not let it out to hurt other people's happiness. Or, if we must speak our wretched feelings, let us go into our own room and lock the door and close the windows, that no ears but our own shall hear those hateful words.

The Peacemaker's Beatitude

❧ *I*t is very easy, if you are talking to one who has a little distrust of another or a little bitterness against another, to say a word to increase the distrust or add to the bitterness. We like to approve of the one with whom we are speaking, and in doing so we are apt to confirm the bitterness or sense of wrong from another. Let us be on our guard that we do not unintentionally widen little rifts into great breaches. Let us seek always to be peacemakers. There is no beatitude whose blessing is more radiant than that of the peacemakers—"they shall be called the children of God."[18]

The Blessing of Struggle

❧ *T*he daily temptations that make every true life such a painful conflict from beginning to end bring us constant opportunities for growth of character. To struggle is to grow strong. The soldier's art can be learned, and the soldier's honors can be won only on the field of battle. If you would grow into the beauty of the Master, you must accept the conflicts and fight the battles. You can live easy if you will by declining every struggle, but you will then get little out of life that is truly noble and worthy. The best things all lie after the battle: you must fight your way across the field to get them. Heaven is only for those who overcome. No one gets the crown without the conflict except those who are called home in infancy and early childhood.

Conscience in Little Things

➤ *S*crupulous people are often laughed at. "Why be so particular? Why be so conscientious about mere trifles? Why be so exacting and punctual in doing small duties?" The answer is that in the matter of right and wrong nothing is little; certainly nothing is insignificant. Duty is duty, whether it be the smallest or the greatest task. You are on the highway to nobility of character if you learn to be scrupulous concerning the smallest things. He that is careful in little things rises a step higher every day. He who is faithful in little things is then entrusted with larger responsibilities. It is the small segments in life that are most important. Look after the little things, and the greater aggregates will be right. Make the minutes beautiful, and the hours and days will be radiant.

Goodness in the Shadows

Shall we trust our Father only when our lives are filled with pleasant things, and then not trust Him also when a shadow falls over our hearts? Do you think God is good only when He makes all things please you? Our call is to trust God at all times. For even if sorrow should enter our home, He is able, even in the midst of sorrow, to make our home life sweeter, purer, and more Christlike. If we believe in God, then the shadow will be as rich a blessing to us as the light, and the sorrow will be steps upward on which our feet may climb toward God.

The Cost of Being a Blessing

~ *W*e must live purely ourselves if we would be able to bless others. We must resist sin, even to blood, if we would teach others how to be victorious in temptation. We must bear trials and endure sorrows with patience, submission, and faith, in order to be victorious, if we would become comforters and helpers of others in their trials. You must learn before you can teach, and the learning costs you much. At no small price can we become true helpers of others in this world. That which has cost us nothing in the getting will not be any great blessing to any other person. It is only when we lose our life and sacrifice it to God, that we become deeply and truly useful.

Making Others Happy

    The world needs happiness. There is a great deal of sadness everywhere. The Bible is meant to make people happy. Joy bells ring through it. The mission of the gospel is to create joy. The angel's announcement of good tidings of great joy goes forth today on every breeze. The love of Christ changes darkness to light, despair to hope, tears to laughter, sorrow to rejoicing, in every land. It is the mission of every Christian to be a happiness maker. We have the power to add some gladness to the world. We can do this in a thousand ways— by being joyful Christians ourselves, making our lives a sweet song; by telling others the joyful things of the Word of God; by being kind to all we meet; by comforting sorrow, lifting burdens from others, cheering away sadness and weariness, and scattering blessings wherever we go.

Our Heart—Christ's Kingdom

~ Religion is not an art or a science; it is a life. It is not a mere learning and following of a set of rules. It is the growth of Christlikeness in the heart, spreading then into our whole being. The kingdom of heaven is set up within us, under the authority of Christ, the fount of life. "Christ liveth in me,"[19] St. Paul says. The Christian life is the personal reign of Christ in the heart of everyone who accepts Him. The conquest is slow; the heavenly King finds His kingdom under alien sway. To get full possession and to reign supreme and alone, He must subdue the whole of the old nature. It is this work of submission that is not complete until the believer journeys into heaven. We should harness all the energies of our being toward the bringing of our heart, mind, and will into complete subjection to our King.

Uplifting Power

Has Christ's friendship been to you as close, personal, tender, constant, as the human friendships that have been dearest to you? The close friends of Christ have found no other influence so strong as His precious friendship in forming and transforming their lives. Continually before them in all its purity and spotlessness, in all its strength and heroism, in all its gentleness and beauty, that beautiful Life has shone, a pattern from the mountain let down from heaven for mortals to fashion their lives after, winning them by its loveliness. No one who has had Christ for a friend in any true, real sense has failed to be blessed by Him in the way of growth into a nobler, richer life.

Immortal Work

~ *N*othing found in the material
world is immortal, for matter is perishable.
The noblest monument of every earthly
builder will crumble; but those who work
on the unseen or the spiritual leave marks
that shall endure forever. The touch of
beauty you put upon a life yesterday by the
earnest words you spoke, by the new attitude you started in the heart of your
friend, by the vision of heavenly purity
you gave in your own life to one who was
with you, will be bright when suns and
stars shall have burned out the blackness.
What we do in immortal lives has immortal benefits. Be wise, therefore, and choose
to do your life's work on materials that
shall never perish. Thousands of years later
you will find the things you have done still
enduring in immortal beauty.

Worldly Motive
in Christian Work

There is a great deal of worldly policy among Christians. Some shrink from duties because they fear the consequences. Others refrain from taking sides on important questions or boldly declaring their beliefs—all motivated by self-interest. Too many professing Christians lack courage to speak about their spiritual interests, fearing rejection. The money question sometimes weighs in the balance. The answer to "How will this affect my business or social standing?" may change a course or action. We all know such worldly policy should have no place among the motives swaying the minds of Christians. The only desire should be to know these: what is right, what is our duty, what is the will of God. To be swayed by any other influence is to be unfaithful to our Lord.

Need for Reserve

Many a great battle is won by the reserves. The struggle is perfectly balanced, and victory is uncertain. Then one side or the other brings up the reserve army, and instantly the question is settled. Life's battles and crises are often determined in the same manner: by reserve resources—or their absence. Our days are not all bright, easy, and free of pain. The course is not always smooth. We are all assailed by spiritual foes and temptations, when victory comes only if we can call our reserves into action. We must all accept tasks and duties that completely overwhelm our ability if we have no more strength to draw on than we have on less challenging days. Blessed are they who have learned to draw on the infinite resources of divine strength. With the fullness of God as a reserve, they can never fail.

The Law of Ministry

$\sim$ *G*od gives us, among the good things, work, conflict, self-denial, and bearing the cross. The central law of Christian life is ministry or serving. Some say, "Our chief end is to glorify God and to enjoy Him forever." Yes, but there is no way of glorifying God except by living to bless the world in Christ's name, to bless others by serving them, loving them, helping them, and doing them good. We are debtors, therefore, to everyone we meet. We owe Him love; we owe Him service. We are not to put ourselves on little thrones and demand homage and service from others; rather we are to do the serving. Christ came "not to be ministered unto, but to minister,"[20] and we should act the same way as our Lord.

Unspoken Prayers

Every thought that flies through your brain is heard in heaven. God hears wishes, longings of the heart, aspirations, and hunger of the soul. Do not grieve, then, if you cannot find words to tell God what you want, if you cannot put into well-defined thoughts the hopes and hungers of your heart. When words and even thoughts fail, pray in silent yearnings, in unutterable longings, and God will understand just as well as if you spoke in ordinary language. Much of our best praying is done when we sit at God's feet and do not speak at all but only let our hearts talk.

Christian Love

The spirit of Christian love, if allowed to work deeply and thoroughly in all hearts and lives, will prevent divisions and alienation among Christians. It will lead us to forget ourselves and think of others, not pushing our own interests excessively nor demanding the first place, but in honor preferring one another. It will make us willing to serve, to minister, to stoop down to wash a brother's feet. It will make us thoughtful, too, in all our acts, in all our manners, in all our words. It will make us gentle, kind, and patient, teaching us to be all that Christ would be if He were in our place.

The Life That Overcomes

We can win others to Christ only by being Christ to them, demonstrating Christ's love in ourselves, by living in such a way that they may be attracted to Christ, and may learn to admire and to love Him by what they see of Him in us. One of the most effective ways of winning souls is through beautiful, gentle, Christlike living. Eloquence of persuasion in a preacher is powerful with sinners only insofar as the preacher's life is consistent with that message. Preaching without love in one's life produces only empty chatter. But where the deep, true love of Christ is, the plainest, humblest words become eloquent and mighty.

Recognition in Heaven

≈ Heaven is the Father's house, a home. Can you imagine for one moment a home in which the members of the household do not know one another? The sweetest, best, happiest, and most perfect earthly home is only a dim picture of the love and gladness found in our home in heaven. Heaven is like a holy home, only infinitely sweeter, truer, and better. Home has been called "heaven's fallen sister." If in the imperfect homes of this world we find we have much gladness in the ties that bind heart to heart and knit life to life, may we not be confident that in the perfect home of our heavenly Father all this gladness will be infinitely deepened and enriched? Love will not be different in heaven; it will be wondrously purified and exalted, but earthly love will live on through death into eternity.

Obedience in Heaven

❧ *O*bedience is what heaven is made of. All the life of heaven is simply perfect obedience. A little bit of heaven comes into our lives on earth when we learn to obey the will of God. Obedience is the mark of royalty. Wherever God finds a soul that is ready to always yield to His will, to do His commandments without question, and to submit to His care without murmuring, there is truly a person that He is ready to crown. We get to be like Christ as much as we learn to obey and do God's will. Heaven comes down into our heart only as we yield our lives to God.

Why So Little Kindness?

We let our friends go through life without enough marks of appreciation. We avoid compliments. We hide our tender interest and our kind feelings from them. We are afraid to give one another words of praise or of encouragement in case we should seem to flatter them or we should encourage their pride. Even in many of our homes, there is a strange absence of good, wholehearted, cheerful words. Let us not be afraid to say appreciative and complimentary things when they are deserved and are sincere. Let us lose no opportunity to show kindnesses, to express sympathy, to give encouragement. Silence in the presence of needs that we can meet is sinful.

Room in a Humble Sphere

❧ When you are tempted to complain and resist the difficulties of your circumstances and the limitations of your place in life, remember that Jesus, even with all His divine life and all His great powers, for thirty years found room in a humble peasant home for worthy living and for service not unfitting to His true exalted character. If you can do nothing but live a true Christian life that is patient, gentle, kind, pure—in your home, in society, at your daily occupation—you will perform in the end a service of great value and leave many blessings in the world. This kind of life is a little gospel, displaying in sermons without words the wonderful story of the cross of Christ.

Love's Supreme Moments

Love in its supreme moments does not stop at giving only a little. It does not weigh and measure and calculate and restrain its impulses. Those people know nothing of love who think Mary's costly deed was strange, who try to explain why she acted so lavishly, so wastefully, when she gave her Lord the highest honor she could bestow upon Him with the rich anointing of perfume. If our love for Christ were only stronger, deeper, and richer, we would not need to have Mary's deed explained; we would not calculate so carefully how much we can afford to give or do for others or God.

The Peril of Failure

    *N*umerous lives with magnificent possibilities have been utter failures because men and women have not gone promptly to serve God at His divine call. They were intended to fill certain places. God made them for these places and qualified them for them; but when they were summoned to their work they excused themselves through one plea or another, and buried their talents in the earth. Let us train ourselves to obey every call of God, unless in our hesitancy, distrust, or disobedience we fail at the mission for which we were made, and find only the doom of the useless in God's universe.

If We Only Knew

We should learn to look at the faults of others only through the eyes of love, with charity, patience, and compassion. We do not know the secret history of the lives of others around us. We do not know what piercing sorrows have produced the scars we see in people's souls. We do not know the pains and trials that make life hard to many with whom we are tempted to be impatient. If we knew all the secret burdens and the heart sounds that many keep hidden beneath their smiling faces, we would be patient and gentle with all people.

The Secret of Peace

~ *P*erfect loyalty to Christ brings perfect peace into the heart. The secret of Christ's own peace was His absolute devotion to His Father's will. We can find peace in no other way. Any resistance to God's will, any disobedience of His law, takes our lives out of His hand, and must disturb the peace of our hearts. No lesson that He teaches ever destroys our peace if we receive it with a willing, teachable spirit, and strive to learn it just as He has written it out for us. If we receive the lessons in the way that our Master gives them to us, we shall make our life into beautiful music, and we shall find peace.

Prayer in Sorrow

"Being in an agony he prayed,"[21] is the record of our Savior's Gethsemane experience. Like a bright lamp, this Scripture shines amid the olive trees of that garden to show us the path to comfort in our time of sorrow. Never before nor since has there been such grief as the Redeemer's that night, but He found comfort in His prayer. His agony lessened as He prayed, until at last its bitterness was all gone, and sweet, blessed peace took its place. The gate of prayer is one of comfort. There is no other place for help. We learn from our Lord's Gethsemane how to pray in our own Gethsemanes. God never blames us for asking to have the cup removed nor for the intensity of our prayers; but we pray with submission to His will. When we say, "Not my will, but thine," comfort comes and then peace.

God's Unusual School

No books nor universities can teach us the divine art of sympathy. We must be strongly tempted ourselves before we can understand what others suffer in their temptations. We must have sorrow ourselves in some form before we can be true comforters of others in their times of sorrow. We must walk through the deep valley ourselves before we can be guides to others in the same shadowy vales. We must feel the strain and carry the burden and endure the struggle ourselves, and only then we can be touched with the feeling of sympathy or can give help to others in life's stresses and overwhelming needs. So we see one compensation of suffering: it prepares us for being helpers to others.

The Greatness of Duty

No one can do all that she knows she ought to do or that she wants to do. Yet when we have done our duty, faithfully and earnestly, according to the light and the wisdom given to us, we should not regret afterward if it appears that we might have done things with more wisdom or with greater skill. We cannot get the benefits of experience until we have already gone through the experience. We cannot have an elder's ripe wisdom in the days of our youth. We are able to see when a day is done how we might have lived it better. We should bring to every hour's work our finest skill, our best wisdom, our purest strength, and then feel no regret even if it does not seem well done. Perfection is always an unreached goal in this life. Duty is always too large for us. We can never do more than a portion of it.

The Test of Amusements

❧ *I*s the love of pleasure growing on you, gaining the power and authority over you? Is it dulling the keenness of your zest for spiritual pleasures? Is it making Bible study, prayer, communion with Christ, and meditation upon holy themes, less sweet enjoyments than they once were? Is it making your hunger for righteousness, and for God, less intense? Is it interfering with the comfort and blessing you used to find in church services, or in Christ's work? If so, there is only one thing to do—to hurry to return to God, to abandon the pleasure that is imperiling your soul, and to find in Christ the joy the world cannot give and that never harms any aspect of life. We must test all our pleasures by this rule: Are they helping us to grow in spiritual beauty?

Living to Serve

❧ *T*rue life, wherever it is found, is ministry. Some think they climb the ladder in life as they get beyond serving; but it is the reverse. "Not to be ministered unto, but to minister,"[22] our Lord gave as the central aim and desire of His life. These words proclaim the ideal for all Christian life. The whole of Christ's wonderful biography is focused and summarized here. He Himself holds up the perfect image for the pattern on which every disciple's life is to be fashioned. No one really begins to live at all in any worthy sense until selfishness dies, and he begins to serve others. We should ask, as far as others are concerned, not how we can use them to advance our interests and our welfare, but how we can do them good, serve them, and become in some way a blessing to them.

Making and Keeping Friends

∽⍿ *M*ake friends who are worthy of friendship. It costs to do this; and we can have friends only by giving our lives for them. Selfishness never wins a friend. We can make others love us only by truly loving them. The greatest service wins us no real friends if we do not show love. Rather, our friendships should be beautiful enough for acceptance in heaven. God will never be jealous of pure human affections. Even the brightness of Christ's radiance will not eclipse the faces of the earthly friends we shall meet on the golden streets. Loving God supremely will not drive out of our hearts the love of dear ones knit to us during the years of earthly fellowship in joy and sorrow. The better we love Christ, the deeper, purer, stronger, and more tender will be our love for human friends made in Christ's image.

Weaving Our Soul's Garments

In this life, we are forever throwing the weaver's shuttle back and forth, each moment leaving one new thread in the web of our life forever. Every thought, feeling, and motion, every light fancy that enters only for a moment in the soul, becomes a permanent thread in our lives. Our words and acts are clean and beautiful threads or stained and blemished ones, according to their moral character. Our souls wear this garment for eternity. How important it is that we use only threads of immortal beauty! If we do God's will and train ourselves to think His thoughts and receive the influences of God's love and grace and yield always and only to God's Spirit, we shall weave a seamless robe of righteousness that is radiant and lovely when all earth's garments have faded and crumbled to dust.

Life's Real Problem

The problem of sailing is not to keep the vessel out of the water, but to keep the water out of the vessel. In the same way, the problem of true Christian living is not to keep ourselves out of life's cares, trials, and temptations, but to keep the cares, trials, and temptations out of us. As the sea is the normal medium for ship sailing, so cares are the normal element of life in this world. But we must keep the sea out of our heart. Some people make the mistake of letting their cares and worries creep into their souls. The result is that they grow discontented, fretful, and unhappy. The secret of peace is to keep your heart free from care and anxiety even in the midst of many internal trials. We can only have this secret by opening our hearts to Christ.

Not in Vain in the Lord

We must not measure life by any earthly standard. There are lives the world crowns as successful but that Heaven rates as failures. And there are other lives some may pity, but, in God's sight, are noble successes. Earnest Christians bless others truly for Christ, but there may seem to be little result. Yet we do not know what good may come out of a true work that has at first appeared to fail. "Your labour is not in vain in the Lord."[23] Results may not come immediately, but they will somewhere, sometime. Outside the mill, a waterwheel turns and seems to accomplish nothing. But inside, machinery makes flour to feed the hungry. Our lives may seem, with all their activities, to produce no result, but who knows what blessings they shall become, what impressions they leave on other lives for eternity?

Doing God's Will

➣ Doing God's will builds up
character in us. It builds up in us that
which shall never need to be torn down.
"He that doeth the will of God abideth for
ever."[24] Every act of obedience of our lives
adds a new touch of beauty to our soul.
Every true work we do in Christ's name,
though it leave no mark anywhere else in
God's universe, leaves an imperishable
mark on our own life. Every deed of kindness or unselfishness that we perform,
with love in our hearts for Christ, may not
bless another soul in all the wide world
but will leave its blessing on us. We are
sure, therefore, of getting a blessing in our
own life when we are obedient, even
though no one else benefits.

Giving to Beggars

To the blind man begging by the wayside, to the poor wretch who comes to our door for aid, to the crippled old woman who sits muffled up on a doorstep and holds out a wrinkled hand, we owe something if we are Christians. We may not wish to give money—usually we should not give money—but we ought to give something. We represent Christ in this world, and we ought to treat every such case of need and misfortune as our Master would do if He were standing in our place. We ought to give at least a patient answer, a kind look, and sympathetic attention.

How to Know Christ

To some people, Christ is a creed and a pattern of life, but not a personal friend. There are many who know well the "historic Christ," but to whom He is only a person who lived two thousand years ago. They think of His sweet life as only a vanishing dream; if they realize His resurrection, He is to them an absent friend, like a dear one journeying in another land—real, loving, true, and trusted, but still far away. But all who have limited faith miss the sweetest blessedness of knowing Christ. He does not belong to the past nor dwell far away but is a friend. No mother meant so much to her child as Jesus would be to us if we would let Him. Trust Him and obey Him, and you will learn to know Him and love Him.

Nothing Good Comes Easily

Unselfishness, even in its smallest acts and effects, costs some sacrifice. Work for others that costs us nothing is scarcely worth doing. It takes our heart's blood to heal other hearts. It is those who sow in tears that shall reap in joy. Take easy work if you will, work that costs you nothing, give only what you will not miss, spare yourself from self-denial and waste and sacrifice; but do not be surprised if your hands are empty in the harvesttime. We must give if we are to receive; we must sow if we would reap.

God's Storehouses

Each step in the life of faith is toward richer blessing. Are you God's child? There is nothing before you in the known future but goodness. Every new experience, whether of joy or sorrow, will be a new storehouse of goodness for you. Even in the heart of disaster, you will still find goodness. Even your disappointments will reveal truer, richer blessings than if your own hopes had been realized. Here is a lens through which every true Christian may see his own path clear to the end— from goodness to richer goodness, from glory to glory, the last step through the opening door of heaven into the presence of the King.

Bruised Reeds

Christ is building His kingdom with earth's broken people. Men want only the strong, the successful, the victorious, the whole, in building their kingdoms; but God is the God of the unsuccessful, of those who have failed. Heaven is filled with earth's broken lives, and there is no bruised reed that Christ cannot take and restore to glorious blessedness and beauty. He can take a life crushed by pain and sorrow and make it into a harp whose music shall be all praise. He can lift earth's saddest failure up to heaven's glory.

Opposition—a Means of Grace

Spiritual life needs opposition to bring out its greatest possibilities. It flourishes most luxuriantly in adverse circumstances. The very temptations that make our life full of unceasing warfare train us to be true soldiers of Christ. The difficulties of our experiences, which seem to us to be more than we can possibly endure, are the very school of life for us in which we learn our best lessons and grow into whatever beauty and Christlike character we attain.

Life's Possibilities

⮕ *T*hink of all the magnificent
power God has put into these lives of ours.
He has given us minds to think, to reason,
to imagine, to roam amid the stars, to
wander into the very borders of infinity, to
climb the golden stairs of faith even into
the midst of heaven's brightness. He has
given us hearts to feel, to suffer, to rejoice,
and to love. He has put into our beings the
possibilities of the noblest achievements
and the loftiest attainments. What a shame
it is for one born to live in immortal glory,
called to be a child of God, to become like
the Son of God, yet to be content with a
poor earthly life and to live without reaching up toward God and heaven!

On Soldiers' Graves

As we enjoy our national blessings and comforts, remember what they cost those who won them for us, and those who have conserved them and passed them down to us. We place flowers on the graves of our soldiers who fell, and tell in song and speech of their heroic deeds. Never let gratitude die as we think of the blood that was shed in saving our country. But gratitude is not enough. This redeemed country is a sacred trust in our hands. We are the preservers of its glory. There are battles to fight—for national honor, truth, purity, righteousness, and religion. While we honor patriots, let we ourselves be worthy soldiers in the great spiritual war that never ceases, loving country more than party, and truth and righteousness more than political favor and reward.

Mastering Misfortune

⇌ *A*n Englishman persecuted in prison was cheered an hour every day by a little spot of sunshine on his dungeon wall. Through a grating, the sun's rays briefly streamed into his cell. With the crude tools of a nail and stone, he carved on the wall a rough image of Christ upon His cross. He mastered his misfortune, getting a blessing out of it. No matter how calamity or disaster builds its dark, gloomy dungeon walls about you, never let despair lay its chilly hand upon your soul. No dungeon is so deep that God's love cannot stream through. Carve on the wall of your heart the image of Christ. Master your misfortune, and make it give you a blessing. If you let trouble master you, it will leave a permanent scar upon your life. But conquered calamity becomes your helper and leaves beauty on your soul.

Beauties of Nature

They miss many a tender joy who do not have a heart in sympathy with nature. They lose many a whisper of love that drops from God's lips who do not have ears open to hear the voices of nature. They fail to see many lovely visions of beauty who have not learned to use their eyes in admiring the exquisite things that God has scattered everywhere in such glorious variety. Yet most of us walk amid these inspirations, these rare pictures, these sweet voices, and neither feel nor see nor hear them. God meant us to get comfort and joy from the lovely things with which He has filled our earth.

Failing in Our Little Part

God is not so limited in His resources of power that if one human somewhere fails to do His appointed duty, then His great cause will be defeated. He has large plans, in which the humblest of us have our own allotted place and part. But there is no compulsion brought upon us. We can refuse to do our little piece of work if we choose. God's plan will still go on without us, and other hands will do what we refuse to do. The only effect of our failure in the duty assigned us will be in ourselves. Our own hearts will be hurt by our failure to do our duty, and we shall be set aside, missing the honor and blessing that would have been ours had we done our part.

Leaving All to God

As we go through life, we learn more and more to doubt our own wishing and choosing, as we see how little really comes from our own ways and plans. We learn not to choose at all for ourselves, but to let God choose for us. No doubt we miss heavenly blessings at times, because we do not have faith to receive them in their disguise of pain or grief, preferring our own way to our Father's. Then God sometimes lets us have in our willfulness what we persist in choosing, just to teach us that our own way is not the best. We learn at last to plead, "Bless me, my Father," not daring to tell Him what way the blessing should come, but preferring that it should be as God wills.

As We Forgive

We should not keep count of offenses and forgiven acts, and the time should never come when we shall say we can forgive someone no more. When we are hurting from some injury done to us by another, and when our feeling of resentment is burning like a flame within us, we should remember that the wrong we have done to God is infinitely greater, and that He in His love has freely forgiven us. Should we not, then, be willing to forgive others their little offenses against us? This is why our Lord put into the prayer He taught His disciples the words, "Forgive us our debts, as we forgive."[25] He wants us always to remember that we ourselves need forgiveness, and that if we would be like Him, we must forgive as He does.

The Blessing of Assurance

➤ *E*very Christian's privilege is to
enjoy unbroken assurance of His love
while living close to Christ. God wants us
to trust Him just as fully in the shadows as
in the sunshine. There is grace enough in
Christ to give light and joy to the darkest
experience. Yet it is also true that many of
God's noblest saints, in all ages, have had
seasons of depression, when they lost the
joy of salvation, and could not speak tri-
umphantly of their hope. It is true, also,
that there have been many devoted
followers of Christ who throughout their
life could not get beyond the mere hope
they were Christ's disciples. Is this the best
that the love of God and the grace of
Christ can do for those who are saved?

I Am Ready

Whatever command God gives, we should instantly and cheerfully answer, "Yes, Lord; I am ready to obey."[26] It is not hard to say "Yes" when God leads us in pleasant paths, where the flowers are plentiful, where the way is smooth and agreeable. But we know that sometimes the path is covered with thorns and is rough and steep or runs through fire or flood. We are still called always to say, "Yes." If God calls us to some trial or crossbearing or sacrifice, our answer should always be the same. We should be able to trust Him when our eyes cannot see blessing or goodness in the way He takes us. Every path of God leads to rich joy.

Choice of Friends

We should choose friends whom we can take into every part of our life, into closest fellowship, into each holy joy of our heart, into each work and service, into each hope, and at every point be in sympathy. We ought to accept only the friendship that will bring blessing to our lives, that will enrich our character, that will stimulate us to better and holier things, that will weave threads of silver and gold into our web of life, whose every influence will be a lasting blessing.

Life's Opportunities

All our days come to us filled with opportunities for gathering knowledge and for growing wise, opportunities for growing in character and for becoming stronger, truer, purer, nobler, more Christlike. There are opportunities for doing heroic things for Christ, for performing caring ministries, and for rendering sweet services in Christ's name to those who need loving sympathy and deeds of kindness. Opportunities come to everyone, and they continually come on all the ordinary days and oftentimes in the simplest common things. Yet the trouble with too many of us is that we do not improve upon them and do not seize them as they arrive.

Victory by Standing

≈ *O*ne of the first things in military training is to learn to stand your ground. Old soldiers will tell you that there is nothing that so tests courage and obedience than being required to stand still on the field and hold a position in the face of the enemy. Oftentimes the battle depends on simply standing firm. The same principle applies in all of life. Much of Christian duty is not active, bustling work, but quiet, patient waiting. There come many times in the experience of each of our lives when victory can be gained in no other way. We must stand still and wait for God. Immeasurable harm is brought about in personal lives and hinders the work of God, because we are impatient and cannot wait for the divine call to go forward.

Power of the T

❧ *T*he tongue's power to bless others is simply beyond our understanding. It can impart valuable knowledge, making others wise. It can utter kind words to comfort the sorrowful or cheer the downcast. It can verbalize thoughts that will arouse, inspire, and quicken heedless souls, and even revive dead souls to live. It can sing songs that will live forever in their influence and ministry. We should consecrate such power to God and keep pure for Him. The lips that speak God's name in prayer and Christian song and speak vows of fidelity to Christ should never defile themselves with any type of corrupt speech. They should be kept only for Christ.

dividual Character

≈ Character is personal. It is not a possession we can share with someone else. We can give a hungry person part of our loaf of bread; we can divide our money with one who needs it; but character is something we cannot give away or transmit. The brave soldier cannot share his courage with the pale, trembling recruit who fights by his side in the battle. The pure, gentle woman cannot give part of her purity and gentleness to the defiled and hardened woman she meets. Character is our own, a part of our very being. It grows in us over the years. Acts repeated become habits, and character is made up in the long run of those habits that have been repeated so often that they become a permanent part of our lives.

Work for Others

We can do our best work always when we do it not for ourselves but so that it may bless others. If the motive in all ambition, all toil, all effort, is to become wiser, stronger, greater, and more influential, in order that we may do more in Christ's name for others, then whatever we do will be beautiful and noble. The motive exalts and makes noble the work. We get the largest measure of good for ourselves from our actions when our first aim is to do good to another. If you wish to get the best from any good thing, receive it from God and then quickly minister it in Christ's name to others. The richest blessing comes not in the receiving, but in giving and doing.

Secondhand Bible Truths

Many Christians have their heads stored full of catechism, creed, and Scripture and yet when trouble comes, they have not one truth on which they can really lean or trust their weight, or that gives them any actual support or help. Piles of doctrines, but no shepherd's rod and staff to lean on in weakness; lamps hung up in great numbers but not one of them burning to throw its light upon the darkness; bundles of backpacks tied up in creed and text, but no staff to walk with over the dark mountains. Let us learn to study the Scriptures for ourselves, and to know what we should believe and why we should believe. Secondhand Bible truth is not the kind of food our souls need.

Misreading Events

We are apt to interpret God's provisions in accordance with our own desires. When we are wishing to be led in a certain way, we are quite sure to find signs that seem to favor our own preference. We must be careful to correctly interpret the meaning of events and circumstances. We are not to enter every door that is thrown open before us. The devil opens doors of temptation, but we are not to call opportunities to sin guiding directions from God. His voice in circumstances never contradicts the voice of His Word.

Keeping a Child's Heart

We ought to keep our hearts warm and full of kindness and sweet human tenderness, even through the harshest experiences. Many of us find life hard and full of pain. We meet misfortunes, serious trials, and disappointments. We should not allow these difficult experiences to deaden our sensitivities or make us stoical or sour. Nothing but the love of God shed abroad in us by the Holy Spirit can keep any of us in such gentleness and tenderness amid the grim and severe experiences of life. Yet it is possible to carry the gentle heart of a little child through all life's hardness and frost into a full and ripe old age.

Setting Pain to Music

    In Marble Faun, Miriam, the brokenhearted singer, puts into song the pent-up grief of her soul. This was better than if she had expressed it in a wild shriek of pain. Christ teaches us to set to music our deepest and saddest experiences. We should sing about even our heart's bitterest anguish. It gives us anthems rather than dirges for the expression of our deepest grief, because it reveals something of beauty and blessing in every dark hour, something other eyes cannot see. It lets us hear in our deepest trials the voices of divine love, encouraging, cheering, and assuring us. Surely the lesson is worth the learning. It is nobler to sing a victorious song in time of trial than to lie crushed in grief. Songs bless the world, and they honor God. It is better for our own heart, too, to put our sorrows and pains into songs.

Divine Discontent

The ideal Christian life is one of unquenchable thirst, of bottomless yearning, of divine discontent, wooed ever on by visions of new life, new joy, new attainments. The trouble with too many of us is that we are too satisfied with ourselves as we are. We have attained a small measure of peace, of holiness, of faith, of joy, of knowledge of Christ, and we are not hungering for the larger possible rewards. Pray for discontent with your spiritual state! With all the infinite possibilities of spiritual life before you, do not sit down on a little patch of dusty ground at the foot of the mountain in restful content. Do not be content until you reach the mountain's summit.

The Power of Faith

God can use very weak and imperfect channels of His grace. He can do great things with poor instruments. But there is one kind of person He will not use. He will not send blessing to the world through an unbelieving heart. If you would be a vessel fit for the Master's use, you must have faith. Believe in Christ. Believe that He is able and willing to do the "greater things" He has promised to do through His disciples. Open your heart to receive Him and all that He brings. Expect Him to do great things through you. If we have faith, there is no limit to what Christ will do for us.[27] Faith puts our abilities in Christ's hands, as the chisel lays itself in the hands of the sculptor for the carving of the marble statue.

Blessed Are the Peacemakers

There are enough causes to separate people and to produce friction and alienation. Let us not add to the world bitterness and grief by ever encouraging strife or putting a single coal on the fire of anger. Rather let us try to heal people's friendships. The unkind thoughts we find in another's mind we should seek to change to kind thoughts. We can do no more Christlike service in this world than habitually and continually to seek to promote peace, to keep people from drifting apart, and to draw friends and neighbors closer together in love.

Whatsoever Things Are Lovely

We become truly beautiful to the degree that we become like God. Human morality is not always beautiful. There are people who are good but not lovely. Their "goodness" still has qualities that repel others. But true holiness is attractive. We ought to make our religion so beautiful that all who look upon us shall be drawn to our Master. We dishonor Christ when we claim to be His people and yet show in our character, disposition, and life things that are not in God's character. How will people of the world know what true religion is if you and I do not show them its beauty in our lives? We should seek not only whatsoever things are just and true and honest, but also whatsoever things are lovely.[28]

Love for the Brethren

It is easy enough to love some people—people with tastes like ours, people who belong to our "set," people who are particularly kind to us. But that is not the way Christ wants us to live and to love. True Christian fellowship receives all the followers of our Lord, all who bear His name. We will be known as disciples by our love for one another. It requires grace to love all Christians. We must have the love of God in our hearts before we can love others. We must be close to Christ before we can be close to one another. We must cultivate the thoughts and feelings appropriate for disciples of Christ. The humblest believer is our brother or our sister. Because we are Christians, we are one in Christ.

Between You and Your Neighbor

Let us learn to seal our lips forever on the wretched, miserable habit of telling the world about the speck in our neighbor's eye. Who made us a judge? Tell the faults between you and your neighbor alone. You can find chapter and verse in the Bible for that. Tell the faults, if you will, with love and sympathy in your heart, confessing your own in the meantime. Tell faults because you want to help your neighbor to become nobler, lovelier, and better, because you cannot bear to see your neighbor suffer, not because you want to humble him or glory over her. Tell faults in secret if you are ready for such holy work; but do not tell the world of these faults.

Christlikeness at Home

Keep the lamp of love shining day after day amid the many home cares and duties, amid the criticisms, sarcasm, and thoughtlessness of time, amid the thousand little irritations and arguments of home life that tend to break peace and disrupt a sweet temper. Let your love at home be of the kind that never fails. Wherever else, far away or near, you pour the bright beams of your Christian love, be sure you brighten the space close about you in your own home. No goodness and gentleness outside will atone for lack of love at home.

Getting Ready for Temptation

We must all meet temptation, and the tempter comes so suddenly and so secretively that if we cannot instantly repel his assault, we shall be defeated. There is nothing like texts of Scripture to drive Satan away. We need to have our quiver full of these polished shafts, these invincible darts, and to keep them ever ready to shoot on a moment's notice and to hurl at our enemy. The only way to do this is to make the Word of God our daily study, storing in our memory its precious texts, its counsels, promises, warnings. Then we shall never be surprised, unprepared or defenseless, but for every temptation shall have a dart ready to draw and hurl at our adversary.

The Love of Christ

God puts something of Himself into every human life. He helps and blesses us through our friendships, but these are meant only to draw us up to Himself. Christ Jesus is the only man in whom we can have eternal trust. All other friendships are only shadows; His is the perfect friendship. Behind the sweet, gentle, human qualities in Him that make it so easy for us to come to Him and rest in Him is the power of the eternal God. When we come to His precious human love, for which our hearts crave and that seems so satisfying, we know that His infinite, divine fullness lies behind the tender warmth of the Son of God. His humanity comes very close to us, and we only need to lay our heads upon its bosom. Then when we lean on Him, we are lifted up in the arms of omnipotence.

Whatsoever Your Hand Finds

✑ Find your work wherever Christ has put you. Do whatever He gives you to do. Strive to be full of Christ; then strive to be Christ to the souls about you that are lost and perishing or that are in need or sorrow. Seek to make one little place in this world brighter, better, and purer. Christ has redeemed you and lifted you up, that you may redeem and lift up other souls around you. If your hand is always ready to serve, you will always find work ready for your hand to do.

Doing God's Will

We are never to be rebellious or slow to submit to God, but we must be sure that we have done all we can before we fold our hands and say, "Thy will be done." There come many experiences, however, in which we can do nothing to change things and can only submit to Him. We must not only strive faithfully ourselves in all things to do the will of God, but must allow it to be done in us, even when it lays us low in the dust, even when it strips us bare and shatters all our joys. This will is to be accepted, too, not with rebellion, with murmuring and complaint, but joyfully and lovingly.

Creed and Life

"It makes only a small difference what a man believes, what doctrines he holds: it is conduct that counts." That is the way some people talk as they sneer at creeds. But it does matter what one believes. Wrong believing leads to wrong living. The heathen worships a god conceived as lustful, cruel, and unholy. The Christian worships a God, who is revealed as holy, righteous, pure, and good, and becomes holy, righteous, pure, and good. Beliefs shape our lives. It is important, therefore, that we know the truths about the character and will of Christ, as our conception of Christ will imprint itself upon our life.

Finding the Good in God's World

    Thankfulness or unthankfulness is largely a matter of what we see. Two men look at the same scene: one sees the defects and the imperfections; the other sees the beauty and the brightness. If you cannot find things to be thankful for today, and every day, the fault is in yourself, and you ought to pray for a new heart, a heart to see God's goodness and to praise Him. A happy heart transfigures all the world around us. It finds something to be thankful for in the barest circumstances, even in the dark night of the soul. Let us train ourselves to see the beauty and the goodness in God's world, in our own circumstances, and then we shall stop grumbling, and all our encounters shall start songs of praise in our heart.

Not Your Work, But You

God wants, not so much your work, but you; at least He wants you first, and then your work. Service from hearts not really consecrated to God is not pleasing to Him. We are in danger of forgetting this in our busy, bustling periods. It is easier to offer God a few easy activities than to give Him our heart. The tendency of the religious life at present is to work, and to serve, rather than to love God. So we need to remind ourselves continually that loving must come before doing and serving. The largest and most noticeable work will find no acceptance with God if our hearts are not His.

The Value of Time

Our days are like beautiful summer fields as God gives them to us. The minutes are blooming flowers and silvery blades of grass and stalks of wheat with their germs of golden grains. The hours are trees with their rich foliage or vines with their blossom potentials of purple clusters. Oh the endless, blessed possibilities of the days and hours and minutes as they come to us from God's hands! But what did you do with yesterday? How does the little acre of that one day look to you now? What are you doing with your time? Every moment God gives us has in it a possibility of beauty as well as something to be accounted for. Are we using our time for God?

For the Sake of Christ

Love toward Christ must be the springboard and inspiration of all duty, heroism, fine achievements, and service to others. "In His Name" is the true motto of all Christian living. Serving others amounts to nothing in Heaven's sight if it is not done for the sake of Christ. The service must be truly rendered to Christ, no matter to whom the kindness is shown, or otherwise there is no glory in it, however beautiful it may be in itself. Things we do from any other motive have no acceptability in the sight of God.

Watch Your Heart-Life

We need to watch our heart-life, for it is in our thoughts, feelings, moods, tempers, and affections, that the turning from Christ begins. We need to watch our inner spiritual state. The world may see no limit to our zeal, our religious activity, our earnest promoting of the truth, and yet there may be not enough prayerfulness, love for Christ, tenderness of conscience, hunger for righteousness, or desire for holiness. Is Christ more to you now than He ever was before? Does His love draw you with an overwhelming sway? Can you say, with Zinzendorf, "I have only one passion, and that is He?" Is your heart right?

Pass on Your Blessing

God does not like to bestow His blessings where they will be hoarded, but He loves to put them into the hands of those who will do the most with them to bless others. The central purpose of authentic living is to be helpful to others. The purposeful life is one devoted to Christ, to be used for Him in blessing others. Lay every gift at the Master's feet, and then, when it has been blessed by Him, give it out to bless others. Bring your barley loaves to Christ, and then, with the anointing of His touch upon them, you may feed many spiritually hungry people with these gifts.

Under God's Orders

Wherever God puts us, He has something definite right there for us to do. There is something He created for you to do in a special way. Every day He brings you into places where you have a definite purpose. Every time we find ourselves in the presence of a need or an opportunity to be helpful, we may well stop and ask if God has not brought us to this place for this very thing. We are always really under orders. Oftentimes the orders are sealed and are opened only as the time goes by. To realize this gives our common life a sacredness that should make us revere God. We need to continually serve our King.

The Beginning of Bitterness

Let us instantly crush the beginning of envy, jealousy, and hate in our hearts, never allowing the day to close with a bitter feeling remaining. The hour of evening prayer, when we bow at God's feet, should always be a time for getting everything right that may have gone wrong with us and in us during the day. Next every injury should be forgiven when we pray, "Forgive us our debts, as we forgive our debtors."[30] Finally every spark of envy or jealousy or anger should be quenched, and the love of Christ should be allowed to flood our hearts. We should never allow the sun to go down on our anger.

Written Not with Ink

➦ *U*nbelievers do not read the Bible nor come to church to hear the minister. All they learn about Christ and the Christian life they must learn from those who bear Christ's name and represent Him. If all church members lived truly consecrated lives—holy, beautiful, separate from the world, loyal to Christ in business, in pleasure, and in all things—it is impossible to estimate what the saving power of the Church would be by true example alone. It is awful to think that professing Christians, by the inconsistencies of their personal lives, lead souls to reject the Savior. We are all responsible for our example to others. Our lives should be New Testament pages that all can read.

Beautiful Living

We do not know, when we are aiming for immortality, by what deeds or words of ours we shall be remembered. It may be the most obscure aspect of our life that shall shine with the most radiant glory. Let us, then, seek to make everything we do beautiful enough to be the epitaph on our gravestone. To neglect the least duty may be to spoil the way in which we are remembered. One opportunity missed may hurt the rest of our reputation. If our hearts are always full of love, our lives will be full of gentle deeds that will please God and bless the world. Then we shall write our names where no floods of years, no wasting tooth of decay, no hungry waves of time eating away the rock we stand on, can ever destroy the record of our good works.

Endnotes

[1] Genesis 22:14

[2] Luke 8:45

[3] Ephesians 4:8

[4] John 14:9

[5] John 21:15

[6] Luke 22:42

[7] John 15:12

[8] John 13:34

[9] James 1:12

[10] Mark 14:36

[11] Romans 5:2

[12] Philippians 4:8

[13] Luke 22:42

[14] Matthew 25:21

[15] John 14:15

[16] Psalm 40:8

[17] John 14:13

[18] Matthew 5:9

[19] Galatians 2:20

[20] Matthew 20:28

[21] Luke 22:44

[22] Mark 10:45

[23] I Corinthians 15:58

[24] I John 2:17

[25] Luke 11:4

[26] Luke 22:33

[27] John 14:12

[28] Philippians 4:8

[29] Psalm 144:15

[30] Matthew 6:12

About the Author

∾ *J*ames Russell (J. R.) Miller, a
highly popular turn-of-the-century author,
wrote 50 books between 1880 and 1913,
which sold millions of copies in both
America and the British Isles. His works
were singled out due to their transforma-
tional quality by William Gladstone,
Prime Minister of England, along with
countless leaders and common folk on
both sides of the Atlantic.

About the Editor

James S. Bell Jr., Editorial Director at Moody Press, is a leading authority on Christian devotional classics. He has updated such works as *In His Steps*, by Charles Sheldon, published by Honor Books. His goal is to bring the great writings from the past into the hearts and lives of a new generation of readers.

Additional copies of this book are
available from your local bookstore.

HONOR BOOKS
TULSA, OKLAHOMA